As a pastor for so many tragedies of life has al\ very delicate. Death has ̲ ̲ ̲ ̲, ̲ ̲ ̲ ̲ ̲ be the loss of a loved one, divorce, deployed military, loss of job or a business, and even the death of a vision. *Called Home* is a book even by its title that sets a tone of hope and trust in God's sovereignty facing the sorrows of life. It is refreshing to have a resource espousing hope when facing a tsunami of overwhelming heartache.

—GOVERNOR MIKE HUCKABEE

I vividly remember calling the Giles family immediately after hearing the gripping news about their son, Micah. I recall telling John over the phone before praying with him that he was at war for the heart and soul of our nation in his work there with the Christian Coalition of Alabama and the loss of Micah was a casualty of this war. I watched from a distance how this family remained in the battle for our culture while picking up the shattered pieces of tragically losing their son. This book has been written with a balanced spiritual tone embracing an eternal perspective while applying a common sense biblical approach to facing the hardest challenges of life.

—DR. M. G. "PAT" ROBERTSON
Founder/Chairman of *The Christian Broadcasting Network*
Founder/President of the *American Center For Law and Justice*
Founder/Former Chairman of *The Christian Coalition*

In 2 Corinthians 1:3-4, the Apostle Paul, under the inspiration of the Holy Spirit, wrote, "Blessed be the God and Father of our Lord Jesus Christ, the Father of mercies and God of all comfort, who comforts us in all our affliction, so that we may be able to comfort those who are in any affliction, with the comfort with which we ourselves are comforted by God" (ESV). Deborah and John Giles are fulfilling this plan of God as they encourage others by telling their own story of suffering and giving glory to the Lord for His faithfulness and comfort through it all. *Called Home* should serve as a reminder to anyone who has gone or may go through a similar journey of heartache and tragedy, that the Lord will be faithful to keep His promises. He promises to go through times of suffering with us and He promises to bring good to our lives as a result of such struggles. All He asks is that we continue to trust Him even though we do not understand why. John and Deborah Giles convey this truth in a very real and personal way in *Called Home*.

—JOE GODFREY
Executive Director
Alabama Citizens Action Program (ALCAP)
& American Character Builders

This book is a spell binding work of art that captures every feeling you could imagine. I lost my twenty-one year old daughter Heather Lynn Alsbrooks in 1998, and I can feel the hurt, the feeling of loss, and the joy in knowing she is home. John and Deborah have done an excellent job in telling Micah's story.

—LYNANN HENAGAN
Lost her daughter in a car accident

Called Home is the touching account of the homecoming of an outstanding young Christian man, Micah Giles. It carries the reader inside the family and the kind of value system that was taught and lived. It recounts the deep sorrow when the news of his death was revealed. It also shares much about the grieving process and the way Christians handle death. The songs, essays, etc. that were written by Micah and his family are both convicting and inspiring. *Called Home* is a strong testimony to the assurance of eternal life.

—JOHN ED. MATHESON, PHD.
Executive Director of the
John Ed Mathison Leadership Ministries

We too have lost a precious son. *Called Home* serves as a road map for anyone who suffers any loss.

—GOVERNOR FOB & BOBBIE JAMES

John and Deborah Giles have written a touching and compelling account of a family tragedy and triumph against incredible odds. This is a book of hope. It is a must read.

—JAY SEKULOW
Chief Counsel, American Center for Law & Justice

John and Deborah Giles have given us a wonderful gift in *Called Home*. No one would want to experience the unspeakable agony of losing a child, especially under the circumstances surrounding their son Micah's death. Yet, in an act of enormous generosity, John and Deborah share with us in a life-giving way the good that has come out of their pain. *Called Home* is a good read, a good story, told by good people. Indeed, reading it will do us all a world of good.

—REV. ROB SCHENCK
President, National Clergy Council, Washington DC
President, Faith and Action in the Nation's Capital

Called Home is the faith-inspiring answer to *When Bad Things Happen to Good People*. In sharing their journey through tragedy, John and Deborah Giles, show how to persevere when the path is rocky, and how to see glimpses of God's grace through the darkness.

—WENDY WRIGHT
Former President of Concerned Women for America

Called Home is a beautiful tribute to Micah, and a wonderful testament of faith in the Lord and all that He will do for us if we just let Him. I finished the transcript in one night, and must say that it has helped me to develop a brighter outlook on life. We have to remember that we are all passing through this life, and if we can make a positive difference, then the world is better for it. I wish you all the success in the world with this wonderful book. It's definitely a must read for those dealing with loss in their lives.

—CINDY RAYMON
Longtime family friend, Wichita Kansas

Called Home reminds us that no matter how great and cruel the suffering, God's love and redeeming grace are greater still. With sincere warmth, candor, and practical counsel, the Giles offer great wisdom to those attempting to navigate the waves of fear, suffering, and death.

—JIM AND JOY PINTO
Co-Hosts of *At Home with Jim and Joy,*
The EWTN Global Catholic Radio Network

Called Home is a book of encouragement for all who suffer loss. It unveils God's great Truth: life reigns over death. Romans 8:28.

—BOB & JUNE RUSSELL
Chairman & Vice Chairman
Christian Coalition of Alabama 1993–2006

Called Home

A True Story of Overcoming
Grief after Losing a Child

Called
Home

JOHN AND DEBORAH GILES

TATE PUBLISHING
AND ENTERPRISES, LLC

Published by Tate Publishing & Enterprises, LLC
127 E. Trade Center Terrace | Mustang, Oklahoma 73064 USA
1.888.361.9473 | www.tatepublishing.com

Tate Publishing is committed to excellence in the publishing industry. The company reflects the philosophy established by the founders, based on Psalm 68:11,
"The Lord gave the word and great was the company of those who published it."

Published in the United States of America

ISBN: 978-1-61862-840-4
1. Biography & Autobiography / Religious
2. Self-Help / Death, Grief, Bereavement
12.05.07

Acknowledgements

A special thanks to Mr. John M. Wise, Sr. of Luverne, Alabama. If it were not for the encouragement and support from Mr. Wise, *Called Home* would most likely not have been a reality. Thank You Mr. Wise.

We want to thank Cindy Raymon, a long time friend we reunited with on Facebook in 2011. After sending her the book she insisted it had to be printed. She emphasized we needed to find a Christian publishing house. The first name I found on the Internet was Tate Publishing and they were the only publisher that I sent the manuscript to. Cindy helped us edit the earlier transcripts of the book.

We would also like to thank Kathy Hammond who was a house guest for a few months after her car broke down in Montgomery, Alabama. She was gifted in editing and grammar and helped us tremendously.

Thank you, Nancy, for lending us your gift of proofreading.

If it were not for Stacey Baker and Dr. Richard Tate, Founder and Chairman of Tate Publishing, this book would not have been a reality. We were not comfortable with the idea of vanity publishing; we wanted the book to stand on its own merit. I will be forever grateful for their affirmation and confirmation that we needed to publish this book. All of the associates at Tate have been the Dream Team to work with. We would also like to thank Nancy Ayers from Luverne, Alabama for helping with the final edit.

—JOHN W. GILES

Table of Contents

37

> "Yea though I walk through the valley of the shadow of death, I will fear no evil."

Psalm 23:4 (KJV)

Introduction

By DEBORAH GILES

Having recently gone through what most people would consider the most horrific event a parent can experience—the death of a child—I felt inspired to keep a journal of how God has brought our family through this experience. The thought of losing a child does cross the mind of every parent; that is why we all seem to be so protective. There are certain lessons we have learned that in our view would help anyone who is facing a major crisis in their life. One interesting point that I have observed is that the level of grief we experience is somewhat determined by how we view death. If death is *the end*, we will probably suffer greatly. If we believe that death is a continuation of this life, we can accept our present situation as temporal and move on with the expectation that we will soon be reunited. I have come to believe that it is this life that is temporal. We will be in the next life longer than we will be in this one. If we can embrace this concept of truth we can truly turn our mourning into rejoicing. One of the goals of this book is to set a tone of hope while journeying through life's most difficult tests.

The year that we lost Micah was filled with tremendous victories and what appeared at the time to be crushing defeats. We have truly learned Philippians 4:12-13.

> I know how to get along with humble means, and I also know how to live in prosperity; in any and every circumstance I have learned the secret of being filled and going hungry, both of having abundance and suffering need. I can do all things through Christ who strengthens me."

And verse 14, "Nevertheless, you have done well to share with me in my affliction." We praise the Lord for the body of Christ who stood with us in our affliction and shared our joys and sorrows. During this one-year period, we housed and cared for my elderly grandmother, saw the defeat of Republican Governor Fob James, for whom John worked, lost a son, were sued for three hundred million dollars, and dealt with a married, Christian woman stalking my husband. At times, the furnace of afflictions seemed crushing. The seemingly endless trials could easily have blinded me to the equally numerous triumphs.

During this time my husband was President of the Christian Coalition of Alabama, which is a 501(c)(4) education and lobbying nonprofit organization. Some of the triumphs we experienced were defeating video poker in our legislature (which caused the three hundred million dollar lawsuit). The gambling interests sued my husband and several other pro-family leaders and the case was thrown out of federal court within minutes after the judge called the court to order. We received two large sums of money from the unexpected sale of some property, which enabled us to become totally debt free. Through the strength of God, the churches in this state defeated a state-run lottery by referendum vote. These are just a few of the victories we witnessed during these turbulent days.

I have always lived life with the belief that as parents we lay down our life to pave the way for our children. The summer after Micah's death, I saw a picture (a vision if you will) of Micah laying face down prostrate, imbedded in the road stretching out before me. I was being shown that somehow Micah's life was paving the way to someplace that the Lord was taking me. Life isn't always what we want, but through Christ, it is always what we need.

Most of the early years of my Christian walk were spent believing that if you saw a scripture in the Bible, you could claim it as yours, confess it, and have it. This type of belief leaves people treating God as their personal butler. I do believe that every promise of God is "yes" and "amen." The only difference now is that I believe that the Holy Spirit must first quicken it. Then I must receive it and stand on it. At this point in my walk with the Lord, I believe that it is presumptuous to grab any scripture I see and claim it for myself. When Jesus was in the wilderness being tempted, Satan quoted scripture, but Jesus held onto the word that the Spirit was revealing to him for that very hour. The Holy Spirit will bring the scriptures to your remembrance as you have need of them. This is the way that we walked through this trial in our lives. I hope that our example of how we heard that still small voice and then acted on it will inspire faith in others.

It is our understanding that what we experienced is not common. That is the reason that I had a desire to journal our experience with hopes that others could benefit. Our God is no respecter of persons, so what he did for us he will do for anyone. People who are experiencing grief and pain need not feel condemnation. "There is no condemnation to those who are in Christ Jesus" (Romans 8:1). It is our prayer that something in our testimony might bring closure and healing to someone's pain. "We overcome the devil by the blood of the lamb and because of the word of our testimony and we love not our lives even unto death" (Revelation 12:11, KJV).

Part 1

Meet Our Family

By DEBORAH GILES

*How else but
through a broken
heart may Lord
Christ enter in?*

—Oscar Wilde

In 1971, I met my husband, John, in our senior English class at Robert E. Lee High School in Montgomery, Alabama. We became best friends. In the fall of 1972 we married. Looking back, I see just how young we really were. That was twenty-seven years ago.

In 1976, having just become the mother of our eldest child, our daughter, Zaviera, I had begun searching for God. The Lord drew me to read the New Testament where I discovered new life. My life has never been the same since the night I knelt beside my bed and prayed to receive Christ as my savior and Lord.

In 1979, our second child was born. We felt inspired to name him Micah Worthington Giles. Micah was always a special child as all of our children are. My grandfather told me many times, "One day Micah will be a great man." Also when Micah was only a few years old, he had a dream where he and Jesus were shepherds watching the sheep together. In the dream, the Lord gave Micah a slingshot (Micah said there were many sling shots there), and Jesus told Micah, "You defend the sheep against the lions, and I will defend the sheep against the bears."

We also have another child named Stephen who was born in 1984. It seems that most of my identity is wrapped up in being a wife and mother. I am very inspired by Deborah in the Bible. In Judges 5:7, she states the qualifications for her call. "Until I, Deborah, arose, until I arose, a mother in Israel." As life goes on, I find that the most important things that I have done in life were to impart natural life and the life of God to my children.

I have never been content to warm a pew in a church. I have always endeavored to follow Jesus wherever He might choose to take me. Since my conversion, life has been full of being a part of the church, having church functions in our home and practicing lifestyle evangelism. In 1989, during a time of prayer and fasting, the Lord began breaking my heart about my selfishness. My life was totally wrapped up in my family and our own lives. He broke my heart as He showed me that "...to whom much is given, of him will much be required" (Luke 12:48). He showed me that there was room in my life for much more. In this season of prayer, He also showed me in a deeper way that I needed to become more involved in the lives of women who were seeking abortions. During most of the 1980s, we had ministered in this arena. We had housed pregnant teens and we had lobbied, written letters, made calls, worked in a crisis pregnancy center, and spoken out publicly in defense of the unborn.

As soon as the Supreme Court handed down the Webster Decision, I knew my call was associated with abortion. Children were dying right here in my city, and no one was weeping for their loss. I saw that no hands were reaching out at the abortion clinic to be His hands. I needed to answer the call of Proverbs 24, verses 10 through 12.

I read Verse 11 first which says, "Rescue those who are being taken away to death, and those who are staggering to slaughter, oh hold them back."

Verse 12 continues, "If you say, see, we did not know this, does He not consider it that weighs the hearts? Does He not know it that keeps your soul? And will He not render to man according to his work?"

I first read Verse 11 and went back to Verse 10, "If you are slack in the day of distress, your strength is limited." He was calling me to arise and shine for my light had come. We are called not just to preach the good news but also to destroy the works of the enemy.

Almost from day one of this call on my life, my son Micah came under attack. It appeared many times that he was my Achilles heel. I was very involved in the pro-life movement against abortion. There were so many times that I almost threw in the towel over the past ten years because Micah came under attack. It seems as though when we are trying to follow God's will for our own life, our family comes under attack as well. On many occasions I would compose a letter in my mind to resign and somehow the Lord would shut the door on my efforts to quit. It was hard to function as director of Sidewalk Counselors of Montgomery with personal heartaches and trials going on in my family.

Micah, like so many teenagers, went into a time of rebellion. Micah was sneaking out of the house at night, stealing his sister's car, drinking, hanging around with other troubled teens and was smoking marijuana like a steam engine. His struggles caused us untold heartache and soul searching. We asked ourselves, where did we fail as parents? Later, I asked Micah, "Looking back, where did Dad and I fail you?" His answer was that the failure was not ours but his. Micah was not shy at all about shouldering the responsibility of his actions. While he was quite the rebel during this time, he was also quite a man to face the consequences of his actions.

During Micah's time of rebellion I tried to be transparent with my friends in the body of Christ. Many of our friends prayed and fasted for Micah. There were times when my friends would come over and pray over his bedroom and anoint it with oil. On several occasions Micah would rebuke me with, "Have you and your friends been in my room praying again?" Micah almost always knew when we were praying for him.

All families have serious challenges. One of the hardest jobs on earth is being a parent and raising children responsibly. What is evident in raising a family, is that no matter how hard we try to be a good witness as a Christian family, the devil does indeed attack our families. All of us know at least someone we respect as a role model parent, and yet even in the best of families, problems and challenges exist.

Micah

By DEBORAH GILES

A man ought to live so that everybody knows he is a Christian… and most of all, his family ought to know.

> —Dwight L. Moody

I remember how Micah, even as a toddler, would raise his hands in praise to God. I believe that Micah had a born-again experience as a young child and was lured off the path of life. Three years before his death, Micah had an awesome encounter with God in his bedroom late one night. His testimony and a collection of Micah's writings are included in his own words later in the book.

Micah's last three years were lived with a zeal for the Lord that any parent would be proud of. This is not to say that Micah did not have his problems. He was very much a man with clay feet like many of God's men. Abraham, David, Samson, and even Solomon had struggles. In some of their situations these particular struggles hastened their deaths. I do not want to magnify his shortcomings within these pages. My desire is to celebrate his life and impart faith to the hearers. I also do not want to canonize my son because from time to time his halo was on backwards. This journal is meant to serve as a demonstration of God's mighty grace that saves through faith and is not based on our own righteousness.

Micah was a very intuitive, inspired person. There were many times during his life, whether he was walking with God or not, that he would come up with some profound inspiration. He had a way of cutting straight to the quick. Many times he reminded me of the men described in Hebrews 11:37-38. "They went about in sheepskins, in goatskins being destitute, afflicted, ill-treated men of whom the world was not worthy, wandering in deserts and mountains and caves and holes in the ground." Micah was an adventurer. His mischief and sometimes restlessness would cause him to wander in his mind and sometimes physically away from home; you know the grass-is-greener theory. I would always tell him, "You need to learn what Dorothy did in the Wizard of Oz, 'there is no place like home'." Looking back now maybe he knew better than me where home really is.

When I had my experience with God in 1989, one of the things that became very real to me was the true meaning of faith. I had always been taught "faith is the assurance of things hoped for and the evidence of things not seen" (Hebrews 11:1). This was only part of the inspiration, the real heart of the matter is found in Hebrews 11:9-10 when the scriptures speak of Abraham.

> By faith he lived as an alien in the land of promise, as in a foreign land, dwelling in tents with Isaac and Jacob, fellow heirs of the same promise; for he was looking for the city which has foundations, whose architect and builder is God.

When we as Christians begin to live our lives as if this place is not our home and realize that we are only sojourners passing through, we will stop "laying up treasures on earth where rust and moths corrupt." (Matthew 6:19).

What at times seem to drive me crazy about Micah could very possibly have been godly ideals and concepts.

He really did not have a place to lay his head. He wasn't particular about having a room, a nice vehicle, or nice clothes. All he really cared about was fellowship with God and men. Nobody could be more handsome than Micah when he was all dressed up in a tux or suit. He was comfortable in those kinds of clothes, but he really enjoyed wearing a working man's clothing. His cousin, Heather, once questioned him about his khaki pants. His khaki of choice was Dickeys. Heather informed him that "mechanics wear Dickeys," which served to confirm his choice. He was always the non-conformist.

Micah was very much the outdoorsman. He would come home, pack up his dog, a sleeping bag, and a snack and head to the country to spend the night; sometimes alone, sometimes with his brother or a friend. As a woman, I could not understand this, "Here you have a nice bed and running water. Why would you want to rough it?" He also enjoyed hunting and fishing with a passion.

Micah had a special girl in his life, Mary Margaret Patranka; she was very much a stabilizing force for him. The day we found Micah's body would have been their three-year anniversary of dating. The first memory I have of their relationship was her delivery of a box of scriptures she had made for him. She put a lot into this project; the box was decorated, and inside were three by five cards with handwritten promises from the Bible. Several times, John and Micah sat in his room reading scriptures from the box.

Micah had bought an engagement ring for her in the summer of 1998. I remember the day he told me he was going to ask her parents if he could marry her. I told him they would say no, but he went anyway. When he came back home and recounted the story he said he had asked her father, Joe, if he could marry his daughter. He said Joe emphatically said no. I asked what her mother, Debbie, had to say. He said she didn't say anything, she just looked on with horror on her face. I tried to tell Micah that a father does not want to give his daughter to a man who does not know where he is going. Micah was not finished with college. He did not have a stable income. All he had were dreams. Mary Margaret had dreams too; she had even begun collecting furniture for their future home.

Our children worked during the summer in order to pay toward their first car. Both John and I felt that if they had no investment in their possessions then they would not value them. Micah's first summer job was at a local nursery doing heavy lawn work. He worked like a slave all day in the hot, Alabama sun and staggering humidity. He purchased his first car with the help of his father. The following year, he got a job working indoors with friends who owned an animal kennel. Sometime during that summer, he cut the owner's mother's lawn. When she paid him, he got to thinking, "Now why am I working at the kennel?" He thought he had found the mother lode. Over the next few years, he would discover that owning his own business was not all that it's cracked up to be.

He came home and took possession of our lawn equipment, and voila! He was in business. Little did he know that residential lawn equipment was not meant for commercial use. Slowly but surely, our equipment failed. Between buying new equipment, repairs, and the expenses that he incurred, he was doing good to simply keep his head above water. His father helped him acquire new commercial equipment piece by piece. Micah's strong drive helped him to be a young entrepreneur.

When it came time to do the actual work, Micah managed to get some help—free help. There was a real Tom Sawyer side to Micah. He could somehow convince his brother or a friend to help him with his work just to have the pleasure of his company. He would even recruit his father on Saturday afternoon to go and help him as well. John always looked at this as a good time to be with Micah, just the two of them; that is unless Stephen wanted to join the fellowship.

Being in business was a wonderful learning experience for him. He not only learned about business but also about God and life. Many of his lessons were hard and expensive. I believe all of his customers would testify that he was always a testimony of some sort when he came by. Micah saw his work as a ministry. His existing customers recalled him being a blessing to them as well. The night we found his body, one of his customers, Kathleen Parsons, came to the house and told us of one of his lawn-cutting trips to their home. He arrived late in the afternoon. Mrs. Parsons had invited him in to visit, which turned into an invitation to dinner. After dinner, as they sat around in the den visiting, he remembered why he had come to their home and went out to cut their grass.

Margo Lorenzo told us about a time when she had purchased a tray of flowers to be planted in her yard. When he asked how she wanted them, she told him to do as he thought best. When she went to view the placement she found them arranged in the shape of a cross.

One of his most difficult lessons came when he had been offered to bid on a new job. He brought in a friend with him to view the work. His friend encouraged him to bid high. Later when he checked back with the man about his bid, the man informed him in no uncertain terms how low he thought of Micah because of the bid. Late that night Micah could not sleep because of their conversation. He called the man and woke him. He apologized for the bid and offered to do the job for free to win back his name. He was given the job, and he was Micah's customer until he sold the business.

Micah's brother Stephen worked many days with him. To this day, Stephen recalls on a number of occasions they would see a lawn that needed cutting. They would stop, cut the grass and leave a Bible with a note that said, "Your debt has been bought and paid in full by the Lord Jesus Christ."

We knew he had established a relationship with someone in the Gideon's organization here in Montgomery because he always had Bibles and tracts. When we cleaned out his truck after his death, we found eight Bibles. We gave these to each one of his pallbearers. Several times, he told us of how he would take men who were asking for money at the local gas station to go get a burger and give them a Bible. Micah learned about alms giving at home. He would use experiences like this to share his testimony and pray with these people.

He really had a heart for the lost. He would fast and pray for them even when he was doing heavy lawn work. I remember one occasion where he was determined to go on a three-day fast. The whole fast took place during a regular work week, and by the third day he became so weak and sick that he threw up in a customer's yard. He drove home, got up to the door of the house and crawled into the house on his hands and knees. When he got into the front door he collapsed on the floor. That picture of him remains in my mind—Micah following hard after God with his whole being.

About a year before his death, he felt that the Lord was leading him to preach the gospel in restaurants. This did not sit well with John and me. We have always taught our children to obey God, but this just did not fit into our neat little God Box. We all have our own God Box as to what we feel like God may want to do versus what we may want to do. I encouraged him to call some of our minister friends for guidance on this issue. There was much division among those that were asked. Looking back, I now believe that God had inspired him to do this. His actions of following the Lord as he best knew how became one of the trademarks of his life that is a bit of a legend in itself to those who knew about this calling to go into restaurants.

The first few times he did this in restaurants, he tried preaching a whole message. He soon found out that you could be thrown out or arrested with this approach. He fine-tuned his message to about forty seconds, which enabled him to slide in and out without much commotion. The scripture that he used was Matthew 7:13-14 (ISV). He would eat dinner, then pay his bill and right before he would leave the restaurant he would whistle very loud. Micah and his father can whistle and you can literally hear it a half mile away. The restaurant would become dead silent. Then he would say, "There is a way that seems right to a man but the end thereof is death. Wide is the gate and spacious is the road that leads on to destruction and many are those entering by it. Because narrow is the gate and contracted is the road that leads on to life, and few are they that discover it. Jesus said I Am the Way, I Am the Truth, I Am the Life." Then he would say, "Have a nice evening and enjoy your dinner." His restaurant message is inscribed on his tombstone.

One day, when we were talking he told me that he really did not enjoy doing this but he said he had to. He was a very bold person, but not a person who was looking for attention. Micah had a very special relationship with his grandfather, W.O. Giles, Sr. W.O. was a wonderful grandfather; he always had time for the children. He was there to give them advice or take them fishing or just sit and visit. Before my father-in-law died, he had a dream in which he introduced Micah in a coliseum full of people as the next John the Baptist. This very much describes what God was doing in Micah's life. Micah at this time in his life would point to Jesus and then say, "He must increase and I must decrease" (John 3:30).

Many times I would tease Micah that he was Jonah. I felt that he was running from God, and I think he had much in common with Jonah. We have touched on previously about why we called him Jonah, but Micah had times where he was running from surrendering his life to the Lord let alone a specific calling on his life. Looking back now, I see that Micah was resisting the box that most people put you in when you live a Christ-centered life. You go to college and get a degree in God. Then some unsuspecting little church calls you, and you begin to try to put into practice all the things that have filled your head. Don't get me wrong. I believe in classroom study, but most lessons are eventually transferred from the head to the heart in the desert and the wilderness.

The week Micah died was an unusual week. Micah worked full time for an electrical company, GT Key (for his girlfriend's father, Joe Petranka), and he went to college at night, so to say he was rarely home was an understatement. That week, he had come down with some sort of infection that made him weak and feverish. Early in the week, we went to the doctor, and they put him on antibiotics. He did not begin to feel better until Wednesday evening. He had class that night, but decided he would rather go with me to church and have communion. Communion was very important to Micah and to our whole family.

On Wednesday evening, we attended the Church of the Ascension, an Episcopal Church around the corner from our home. They have beautiful worship (in the style of "Peter, Paul, and Mary"), a time of testimony, prayer, and communion. Only God knows how precious it was for me to have communion with my son two days before he went home. Several years earlier, I had the same experience of having communion with my father just days before his death. We did not attend the same church, and it had literally been years since we had taken communion together.

My sister in law, Caroline joined us for church that night. Looking back she not only viewed taking communion together that Wednesday night very special, she also mentioned how affectionate Micah seemed that night. She and John came in late and sat behind us and watched as I was rubbing his shoulders and back during church. She noticed Micah was leaning into me with affection as I physically loved on him. It was something mutual between us; Micah certainly enjoyed the affection and I loved giving it to him.

Micah went back to work Thursday, and later that night he drove to Auburn to take Mary Margaret out on a date. I had a very odd experience that night. John was out of the house, and I was home alone. I was surfing the TV channels looking for something to watch and landed on *ER*. I don't remember having ever watched the show before. The show that night was about a car accident where a young man had been burned and was hours from death. His parents were on a trip and driving home as quickly as possible to be with him. The doctors knew the parents would never make it before he died so they put them on the telephone to say their goodbyes. I remember weeping with great emotion as I watched such a gripping human drama, unbeknownst to me that my own life was about to be turned upside down.

Every Friday morning, I sidewalk counseled at the local abortion clinic, so I would leave the house before Micah came downstairs. On his way to work, he usually passed by the clinic and honked and waved, but this particular morning, he stopped to visit. He told me all about his date the night before. He told me how much he loved his girlfriend and how much she meant to him. He also told me about the movie that they had gone to see that night. It was *Patch Adams*. I told him that the previews made it look like a stupid movie to me, and I had no interest in seeing it. He encouraged me that I must see the movie. He also told me he had a date with his girlfriend on Saturday night. This was my last visit this side of eternity with my son.

That night, he came in from work, cleaned up, and went to see his friend Joey because Mary Margaret was not coming home from college until Saturday evening. Micah took our Jeep that night because his truck was in the shop receiving its third transmission. Later, John commented on the look in the eye that Micah gave him that night as he left the house; almost like he knew it was a last goodbye.

Saturday morning when we awoke, John and I noticed that Micah had not come home. I was a little worried because he was in our Jeep. I would not be surprised if Micah did not come home when he was in his truck, but he would not keep our Jeep out all night.

We had, at that time, a Saturday tradition in our family. We would go to Country's BBQ for lunch. So when lunchtime came, I was fearful since we had not heard from Micah. I kept thinking, "Be strong and courageous" (Deuteronomy 31:6). That afternoon, when we got home, I could not get it off my mind. Around five o'clock that afternoon, his girlfriend called. I was quick to inform her that he had not come home the night before. I thought that her rebuke to him for not coming home and causing all of us to worry would be more effective than mine, but I sensed puzzlement and concern in her voice.

About thirty minutes later, Joey called. Joey had attended high school with Micah at New Life Christian Academy. Earlier that year, they had lived together. Joey was calling looking for Micah. Then I was really blown away. I told Joey I thought Micah was with him. At this point, John took the phone to get to the bottom of it. Joey had not seen Micah since the night before when he left him. John left it with Joey to call if he heard from Micah.

We had planned to go ballroom dancing that night, so we went ahead. After we arrived we kept calling our home and Mary Margaret's house to see if anyone had heard from Micah. I knew that Micah might vanish without calling us, but surely he would call Mary Margaret or Joey. By ten o'clock that evening, we were thinking we needed to go to the police.

Missing

By DEBORAH GILES

I know God won't give me anything I can't handle. I just wish he didn't trust me so much.

—Blessed Mother Teresa

We went to the police station to file a missing person's report. We found that when a child is Micah's age, the police do not take you very seriously. They assured us that he had probably gone off to clear his head. I knew this was not the case because our entire last visits with him ended on a good note. John and I left the police station and went home. We went to bed and miraculously slept all night. I awoke the next morning to John saying, "Deborah, he did not come home." John had been invited to speak at a church breakfast by a friend, Hosea Tidwell. After the breakfast, he decided to begin tracing Micah's steps from Friday night, and he had me stay home in case he called or came home. I remember asking the Lord that morning, "Lord, you said in your Word that you do nothing without first revealing it to your servants the prophets. What is going on?" I prayed Romans 8:28. "Lord, you cause all things to work together for good to those who love you and to those who are called according to your purpose. Lord, our whole family loves you, so I know that whatever is happening will be for our good.

During this time John was calling all of Micah's friends. He also began interviewing all the people who saw Micah on Friday night. At this point, the police had not in any way become involved.

I went into the den and decided to watch one of the TV preachers. I turned on D. James Kennedy. He was showing footage of the train wreck that claimed the lives of two precious, little sisters. I knew the Lord was telling me Micah was gone as soon as I saw the footage of the train wreck. I prayed, "Lord, take this cup from me, but not my will but yours be done." I would go through this in order to minister to others from the vantage point of having been there. I argued with him that I would rather learn this from someone else rather than experience this loss first hand. I told him I wanted to learn this with *Cliff's Notes*. The Lord is so patient when we argue with Him. I knew I had to let Micah go.

This was a very sobering day to say the least. I had determined ever since lunch Saturday that I would not eat until Micah was found. I thought about King David when his son was dying. He fasted so he might change the Lord's mind. I was alone most of that day except for a few hours that my friend, Betsy, sat with me. John and the other children drove all the roads looking for signs of the Jeep while I stayed by the phone.

By evening, John returned home and called the city police to see if they had heard anything. You can imagine our surprise to find out that our report had not even been entered into their computers. No one was looking for our son. They assured us that around ten Monday morning, they would get the word out. This was very upsetting to John who tried to shake them into some action but to no avail.

John has never been one to pull strings. We try to go through the proper channels, but our son had been missing for two days at this point, and we wanted help. Earlier that year John had worked for Governor Fob James, so he decided to call one of his friends, Danny Hester, with the Governor's Executive Security, an arm of the Alabama Department of Public Safety. John asked him if we could get the troopers to get a helicopter in the air on Monday to ride the roads looking for Micah. The gentleman said he would see what he could arrange.

Again we were able to sleep all night. We were literally surrounded with the peace of God. That morning, as I was waking up, I could hear the birds singing outside in the backyard. I told the Lord, "Someone needs to notify the birds that my son is missing." It was in this moment, it became clear to me God was in control, even with the singing of the birds. God is never changing; the birds were happily rejoicing and singing even though I thought the world should pause and stand at attention. In that moment the world did not pause and I realized that life would continue whether I engaged in the beauty of the birds singing or not. That was a beautiful encouragement to me. So as a message to all of us facing what appears as an insurmountable trial in life; the birds will be singing in the morning.

John hurried to look out the window to see if the Jeep was home, and it was not. He then began to organize a manhunt. First, John drove our youngest child Stephen to school. Then he unsuccessfully tried to find a friend to comb the roads with him. He drove alone that morning riding all the roads that Micah had taken Friday night and wondering if Micah was in a river or swamp.

Our friend, Leigh Wiatt, offered to call the local media, and get Micah's picture out on the midday news. I felt I needed to straighten the house so my daughter and

I went up to Micah's room. As I was straightening the room, I was struck by how much his room felt more like a hotel room than someone's bedroom. It was almost like a testimony to the fact that he was just passing through. Later, as I was looking at what were really his belongings, I found that they would literally fit into a box. He shared his clothes with his brother who was the same size in everything except for his shoes.

John was in Elmore County organizing a search party. He was able to pull together around forty people. He set up a hub in the Hardee's restaurant in Millbrook, which is about fifteen to twenty minutes north of Montgomery. John had determined that this was not going to be dragged out—we were going to find Micah that day.

That afternoon, my daughter and I drove up to the Hardee's. As we were driving, I got a call on my cell phone from an old friend, Pam Williams. She had heard about the search and called to pray with me. This was the first of many reunions with old friends. As she prayed, my thoughts were distracted by the thought, *Should I tell her that Micah is no longer here?* By this time, I knew Micah was gone.

John organized volunteers with maps and sent them out in pairs with radios and cell phones. While we waited at Hardee's, which was the hub of the search and rescue effort, Betty Varner, a long time friend, joined me at the table. We had not seen each other in years, but word was spreading fast about Micah being missing and she came to be with me. Betty's husband John Varner was our pastor at one time and he dedicated and baptized Micah.

THE WRECK
Tracing the Footsteps

BY JOHN W. GILES

If angels were capable of envy, they would envy us for two things; one is receiving Holy Communion and the other is suffering.

—Saint Faustina

After three days of rigorous prayer and searching for Micah, it abruptly came to an end when I received the call on my cell phone from Sheriff Bill Franklin of Elmore County at 2:45 p.m. Although it rapidly brought a weekend of unanswered questions to a halt, it now opened the door to so many new questions. How did it happen? Were there any witnesses? How did he leave the road? And the list of unending questions continued to build in my mind weeks after the funeral. As Deborah described previously in the book, the wreck site was on bridge number five on the I-65 southbound lane, which I might add was about four miles from home. Four to five minutes from home— this thought gripped me for weeks after the funeral; he almost made it to our home before he was called home.

When we approached the wreck site the day we found Micah, I was initially struck with the notion to go down the hill and inspect the site and see my son. There was an Alabama Bureau of Investigation (ABI) agent waiting to greet us at the top of the hill; his job was to intercept me. They knew I was en route to the site. As Deborah and I stepped out of the car, the agent put his hand up in front of my chest, his eyes filled with horror, and he said "Mr. Giles, you do not need to go down there." It was written in his eyes, and yet I persisted, lurching forward. I asked him why could I not go see my son, he was missing for three days, and I needed to see him. Again, he said, "Please Mr. Giles, trust me, you do not need to go down there." Again I persisted and asked who I needed to get permission from to access the bottom of the hill. He said, "ABI will need to give you permission." Well, that was all I needed to know. I began dialing Danny Hester, who was head of Executive Security, and I knew he could get me access. As the phone rang, I re-evaluated the real importance of descending down the hill. Deborah was telling me I did not need to descend down the hill. By the time Danny answered his cell phone, I had decided to withdraw my appeal to go down the hill. When Danny answered, I thanked him for all of his assistance in finding Micah. Danny handled me with great care, and I told him I had decided to withdraw my request to go to the Jeep at the bottom of the hill.

Sheriff Franklin said he was on his way when he called me at Hardees on my cell phone, so I anxiously awaited his arrival. He told me the wreck was under state investigation and was out of his jurisdiction, but he was coming to the site to see me. We had become a team over the course of that Monday looking for Micah.

The scene, as Deborah previously described, was somewhat chaotic. Law enforcement vehicles from the state and all three counties were present in addition to the Department of Public Safety (DPS) helicopter. In addition, the white, Alabama Forensic Station wagon with black shaded windows was approaching the wrecked vehicle to recover Micah's body from the wreckage. The helicopter was responsible for finding the Jeep and also was used by DPS for aerial photography of the wreck site. DPS conducted two fly overs, one in the morning with the east sun and one in the afternoon with the west sun. What was interesting is that the helicopter could not spot the Jeep in the morning because the east sun cast a shadow over the Jeep from the interstate. The west sun put daylight right on the Jeep which they spotted about 2:45 pm.

The first person to be there with us at the scene of the wreck was Mary Margaret's father, Joe Petranka. He had closed his shop and had his men on the manhunt that afternoon. He ran to Deborah and me and embraced me, and I told him Micah was dead. He sobbed as he told me Micah would have been his son-in-law, and he was grooming Micah to run his business. My heart broke for his loss. Other people who stood with us on the side of the road were Tom and Mary Jim Blackerby who are very close friends. They were on their way out of town to care for a sick relative when they saw the commotion on the side of the interstate. They and another friend began notifying family because the media already had the story, and we did not want family to learn of Micah's death on the TV.

At this point, Micah's brother and sister did not know. Zavie and her husband had gone to a doctor's appointment. She was expecting her first child, which was due that very day. In fact, our granddaughter, Kendall Grace George, was born exactly seven days later to the minute of the time the Sheriff called John and said they had located Micah and the Jeep. Stephen had gone to work that day and had just gotten home. He called my cell phone and was pressing me, and I told him on the phone that the Jeep had been found. I handed the cell phone to John, and he told Stephen his brother was dead. I knew that I must get home to be with him. When we arrived home, John and Stephen embraced and wept. John kept saying to Stephen, "I am so sorry your brother is gone. I am so sorry." Then Stephen said, "I've got to go be with Mary Margaret."

When Sheriff Franklin arrived, Deborah had already left to be with Stephen. About that time, Joey arrived at the scene on his motorcycle. Sheriff Franklin was kind enough to load me in his squad car and ride up to the bridge so I could peer over the side at the Jeep—what a mess. I asked Joey to get into the car and ride with us to look. Of course, Forensic Sciences had already left the scene with Micah's body, so all there was to see was the Jeep, muddy from the plunge to the bottom of the hill.

I cannot begin to tell you how many times I crossed that bridge over the weekend hunting for Micah. I never once saw the tracks where he had left the road. Once I saw the tracks and the Jeep, a completely new set of questions emerged in my mind over the next few weeks and months. I cannot recall the exact conversation, but a friend of a friend mentioned he was the photographer on duty who shot the accident scene. I did not even know these photographs existed until I ran into Tommy Giles who is the state photographer for the DPS at a local Montgomery restaurant. I was then reminded of the third party conversation I had about the photos. I called Tommy after lunch at his office that day and inquired if the photos existed. He said yes and that I was welcome to come and look. I waited a few weeks until I was ready to see the pictures of my son in the Jeep. As of today, I am the only family member who has seen these pictures. Deborah pleaded with me to not go, but all I saw at the wreck site was Micah's driver's license, which was shown to me by the State Trooper, this hardly touched bringing closure for me—I needed to know every detail.

I was not sure I was ready to see those pictures. Some of the aerial photos were very helpful for me to determine how Micah left the road and how he was killed. Some of the photos of Micah in the Jeep were not that appealing, but it helped me to bring some closure to his position in the Jeep and how he died. For some, this may not have been a good project to pursue. But for me, it was a must, and I am so glad I took these steps.

Feeling the Love

By DEBORAH GILES

Do not abandon yourselves to despair. We are Easter people, and hallelujah is our song.

—Blessed
John Paul II

As we began driving, we held each other's hand, and I told him, "We've made it through many things in our twenty-six years of marriage, and we are going to make it through this." Then I had an inspiration from God that we were never to say "what if" or "if only." This proved to be one of the most powerful anchors we clung to, even until today. We pledged that to each other as we drove to the wreck site. Somehow we both knew that our Jonah was going to be in the belly of the whale three days. We finally knew the outcome.

Another point I want to mention that happened to us on the way to the wreck site was that we experienced laughter in our sorrow. We have always kept our home full of humor, believing that "a merry heart does good like a medicine." As we approached the site, there was a helicopter flying over the bridge where Micah had driven off. There were emergency vehicles of every kind from law enforcement agencies in the surrounding three counties. This bridge sits in the corner where three counties touch. We smiled as we commented on the fact that only Micah could loop so many people into his home going and cause such a commotion.

Stephen later told us that when he got to Mary Margaret's house, he had a vision of Micah. In the vision, Micah was wearing white and was seated at a white grand piano. Micah looked at Stephen with his special smile and assured Stephen that everything was going to be okay. From this point on, Stephen had the peace of God and was able to share that peace and strength with others.

That evening was a blur of loved ones in the body of Christ and friends coming just to be with us. It was the beginning of hundreds of acts of kindness. It was quite remarkable how the word spread, but it was on every news station, because Micah had been a missing teen. Phone calls began to pour in from around the country, and John, who was president of the Christian Coalition of Alabama, received a phone call from Pat Robertson. Pat Robertson prayed with John. It meant so much for him to take time and call us.

Some acts of kindness that stand out in our minds are former governor's office colleague, John Mark Kirk, coming with two bags of groceries. There was also a neighbor, John Smith, who came in and embraced us and said, "My driveway is yours as long as you need it and I will have your lawn done for you tomorrow."

Everyone said, "I don't know what to say." Take it from someone who has been there; it's not so much what you say, but it is very important that you come. I cannot over-emphasize how precious a visit is at a time like this. You do not have to have some profound inspiration, just the fact that you cared enough to come by is important. We were deeply honored by a visit in our home from Governor and Mrs. James, Lt. Governor Steve Windom, and other members of the executive, judicial, and legislative branches of government. The outpouring was so abundant.

It did not take me long to see how many lives my son had touched. One of the common threads that ran through these stories was that Micah communicated love to those he knew. Many people would say, "Micah was the first person who would say 'I love you' to me." Micah left this world owing no man anything but to love them and because he would always say, "I love you" in his departure he had no unfinished business with anyone. I think this is the cause of untold sorrow in our world. There are too many things that are left unsaid and then when it is too late, there is no way to finish what was left undone. If you love the people around you tell them now. Don't worry about what they will think of you. All of us need to hear these three powerful words: I love you!

Later on that evening, Stephen and Mary Margaret came to the house. I hugged her and felt inspired to tell her, "This is as bad as it gets. You will never experience anything that hurts like this again." I ached for her. Micah was about to leave my home, and she was to be his future. The pain I experienced was hers. Stephen went upstairs to Micah's room and got the ring that Micah had planned to give her as an engagement ring. He gave it to her, and we were later told that she was having it made into a cross.

This night, we were not fortunate enough to sleep. John and I strolled down memory lane all night, remembering the good times with Micah. The next day, we began making arrangements. This was a strange time for us—we were literally surrounded by the peace of God. This peace also puts you in neutral, where it is difficult to make decisions. It seems others have said you feel numb; this is a very accurate description. It is as though some form of a divine insulation hovers over you during this period. Because my mother had to drive in from Oklahoma, we were not able to have the visitation until Wednesday night.

The ministry that took place in our home in the following days was our first-hand training in 2 Corinthians 1:3-6:

> Blessed be the God and Father of our Lord Jesus Christ, the Father of mercies and God of all comfort, who comforts us in all our affliction so that we will be able to comfort those who are in any affliction with the comfort with which we ourselves are comforted by God. For just as the sufferings of Christ are ours in abundance, so also our comfort is abundant through Christ. But, if we are afflicted, it is for your comfort and salvation.

Our cup was full with the demonstrations from the body of Christ. Some of the many acts of kindness extended to our family included doing our laundry, fixing food, answering the phone and keeping a log, making phone calls, and cleaning our house. My daughter said that my friend, Pam Williams, got the award for most helpful; she came early and stayed late. We didn't really see much of her. She just went about doing all kinds of things behind the scenes.

Our pastor, Father Jim Pinto, went to Forensic Sciences to see Micah's body. He had asked us if he could go and pray over his body. After seeing Micah, he highly recommended we not see the body. We had already made the decision not to see Micah's body in an open casket. After all, it had been in a serious car wreck and his body lay there for three days, decomposing. Remember, this was May in Alabama and we were already experiencing some very warm weather. That was not Micah anyway. It was like a coat that he had taken off and left behind. The real Micah was gone, and that was the son and brother we wanted to remember.

Wednesday morning, we had to go to the funeral home to select a coffin. Knowing Micah's simple and thrifty views on such matters, the selection was simple. We chose a wooden, kosher, Jewish coffin. The funeral home thought it best to have visitation in the chapel because of the volume of phone calls that were coming in. It is our understanding that they hired extra temporary staff to handle the phone calls. This proved to be a wise move. While we were at the funeral home, it was brought to my attention that someone had called wanting permission to come lay hands on Micah and raise him from the dead. Zavie and Stephen both stated emphatically that Micah would never want that. Stephen even went so far as to state, "If you want to really see Micah mad, do that."

After being at the funeral home, we drove over to see Mary Margaret. I had invited her to be a part of any arrangements if she felt up to participating. She had passed on the coffin selection process, so we went by to check on her. As we were driving home, something dawned on me as I remembered John's father's dream of years earlier. I said, "John, Micah was in a white robe, and he was with your father when he was introduced as the next John the Baptist. John, Micah is wearing a white robe, and he is with your father!" Once again the Lord comforted me in showing me that He knew about this day long ago. He was reassembling all the puzzle pieces for me. This time, He was putting the puzzle together not me.

FORENSIC SCIENCE
Putting Together the Pieces

BY JOHN W. GILES

*My longing for
truth was
a single prayer.*

—Saint
Edith Stein

I knew Micah was carried to Forensic Science after his body was found in the Jeep. I received a call from the county coroner the night he was taken in to ask me what level of autopsy I was interested in him performing. The whole conversation was nothing but vapor the next day, but I knew they were going to perform the autopsy on Tuesday and get him to the funeral home late Tuesday afternoon. I was asked who would identify the body as being Micah. I paused and gave Father Jim Pinto's name who was coming to Montgomery the next morning from Birmingham.

That very Tuesday, I recall Robbie Molton, the funeral home director, coming to the house at the same time Father Pinto returned from Forensic Science. This hit close to home for Molton because my daughter often babysat for him and was like family to him. We were visiting with Pinto about his guarded description of his trip to Forensic Science, when Molton came to the door to bring us sign-in books and our burial kit.

His face said it all, and he was literally trembling in his voice and hands. We had already decided before he got there that we were going to have a closed casket for visitation and the service. Remember, Micah had been in the heat for three days, and he was not exactly an easy subject for the funeral home to freshen up. I think Robbie was sweating the fact we would want an open casket. We made it easy on him, and you could see relief come over him and color return to his face as we firmly stated the casket was to remain closed.

Due to swelling, Micah needed a larger suit so I sent Robbie back with one of my favorite suits for Micah to be buried in; that made me feel wonderful for it was only three years prior that my father was buried in one of my favorite suits as well. Robbie said they would have to tailor my suit a bit to fit Micah, but it would be very appropriate. About the only thing Father Jim said was, "His hair is as pretty as I remembered."

A week after we buried Micah, I received a phone call from a lady who used the same orthodontist as Micah, Dr. Fosh Smart. She had told Dr. Smart of this tragedy she witnessed and the two of them deduced that it was Micah's wreck. Dr. Smart encouraged her to call me and relay her account. She called our home about ten in the evening on Wednesday after we had buried Micah. Her name is Marcia Webber, a local art merchant in Montgomery. She said, "Mr. Giles, I was at the scene of your son's wreck about the same time of the occurrence." She relayed that she was in north Alabama on business and was returning to Montgomery late Friday night when the tractor trailer she was following on this section of I-65 under construction swiftly made an abrupt lane change to the left, swerving to miss a parked vehicle in the right hand lane. She was stunned to look up and see the parked vehicle with no lights on, and she too swerved to miss the parked car. She did however see a woman in cut-off blue jeans, barefooted, running down the shoulder of the interstate looking over the guardrail for something. Immediately after gaining her bearing, she called 911 to report this incident to the police. Her landmarks were precise and this was exactly the time and location of Micah's mysterious wreck. I later confirmed her emergency call, and it all checked out. The troopers did go out and survey the report about the parked car and by the time they arrived on the scene, the parked car had disappeared. This breaking news did not help matters because it only created more questions about the wreck that are unanswered even today.

The aerial photos and the tire tracks clearly indicate that Micah was in full control of the vehicle. He did everything right once he left the road; the only question now is how and why he left the road. When Micah left the road, he was trying to inch his way back toward the highway but was blocked by the guardrail and concrete bridge. The Jeep, once it left the levy, was hurled about seventy feet forward and forty feet down. The rear end of the Jeep was beginning to lose traction so when Micah left the ground; the Jeep was somewhat in a nose-left position. When the Jeep hit the ground, it was nose first, it immediately kicked left thrusting Micah into the concrete and steel bridge pylon, bringing the Jeep to an automatic and abrupt halt. I was always on Micah's case about wearing a seat belt, and his friends told me later he always wore a seat belt with them. Well, he did not wear his seat belt on this night, and it was a pretty high price tag. Micah was hurled into the rear view mirror when the Jeep first hit the ground, and when he hit the pylon, the steering column plunged into Micah's rear end thrusting him head first into the passenger door, which broke his neck, and he was killed instantly. I saw one photograph, which no one else in my family has seen, where Micah was laying over the console of the Jeep, curled up asleep, just the way I have seen my little boy so many times. Believe it or not, while this is quite a horrible story, it helped me walk though the final seconds of Micah's life, explaining how he died. We cannot explain one final piece of the puzzle though, how and why did he leave the road.

Tommy Giles, the DPS Director of Photography, who by the way is a distant relative—I believe our lineage is connected somewhere in Mississippi—gave me a sobering fact about the wreck. He pointed out that even though the exterior of the Jeep was badly beaten up; the cabin internally was relatively protected. The Jeep never rolled over, but the impact was probably cataclysmic. Tommy told me he had worked many wrecks in his career, and had Micah worn his seat belt that night, he would be with us today. Although that was tough to digest, our family had already come to the resolution that God is sovereign, and we cannot go to the "what if" scenario. Nothing could bring my Micah back, but two commercials are in this story—wear your seat belt, and Jeep builds one tough Cherokee.

We know the Lord was not asleep on the side of the interstate that night when Micah left the road. Nothing I can discover will change this; however, I am still very curious about the remaining eighteen seconds of my son's life. The account recalled by Marcia Webber leaves us with three possibilities in Micah's decision to leave the road. One, he came up on the stalled car and swerved to spare their life. Secondly, he was accidentally forced off the road, or finally, purposely forced off the road. We still do not know.

The last possibility was that he might have been forced off the road purposely by a paid hit man for the gambling industry. Numerous friends and some law enforcement personnel (not officially in the line of duty but as friends) suggested this was a paid hit on Micah's life. I don't want to think this was even a possibility. In my duties with the Christian Coalition of Alabama, we had just defeated video poker legislation, which stood to net the gambling mafia hundreds of millions annually. Micah was in my Jeep, and it was covered with anti-gambling bumper stickers. Many of my colleagues in the pro-family movement thought this was a hit by the gambling mafia. Other subsequent, unofficial conversations with law enforcement officials led to the same conclusion. In addition, Pete Hannah, a friend and Christian Coalition supporter called and left me with the same conclusion. He was the son of General Hannah who was called in by then Governor Gordon Persons to Phoenix City, Alabama, in order to establish martial law in the 1950s. This martial law came into effect after Attorney General Elect Patterson was gunned down in the street by gambling thugs. Pete who was seventeen at the time recounted to me that the standard operating procedure of the gambling rings is to intimidate and distract. He told me he waited for six months to call me, but he felt Micah's death had all of the ear markings of a hit. He concluded they were trying to distract me from the gambling battle. I must admit this crossed my mind when we found Micah dead; but again, we did not question God's sovereignty, and we could not enter into the "what if" mentality. We are not bitter at anyone if this is true, but if there are people free today who make a living taking human life, they need to serve time and hopefully get some help, let alone be redeemed by the Lamb of God,

Jesus Christ. Although this is one remote possibility that we have chosen not to entertain, it does not bring Micah back, and the real test for us is witnessing God's miraculous power to spare our grief, unnatural sorrow, and pain.

Another incident relative to a possible hit came a little closer to home. For three years back to back, the gambling interest hammering hard to pass legislation was met with our (Christian Coalition's) resistance. One of my employees received a disturbing phone call at Christmas time one day from a frequent flyer caller who always complained about the Christian Coalition and me personally in the gambling fight. He always sounded drunk when he called and routinely left threatening messages on the answering machine saying I needed to leave town and get out of the way of legalizing gambling. Christine Bennett, one of my staff members, froze up and did not tell me about the call, which was a mistake. He called one day and said, "Tell John Giles to get out of town and out of the way of legalizing gambling." He further stated, "We know all of this began when his son Micah was killed on I-65. I don't guess any of us will ever know what happened that night, will we?" I had Christine sign an affidavit of the phone call, and we called in the attorney general's office to review the matter. This guy could be a fluke, but it still caused a lurking suspicion that Micah's life may have been a result of my work. This weighed heavily on me for days. Was I responsible for my son's death? Did my work cause his life to end prematurely? Then, I remembered—no "what if's." This profound inspiration from God given to Deborah has spared us so much potential agony and despair. We tracked down the caller by his number, and it is still undetermined if he has a connection or knowledge relevant to Micah's death.

Another unanswered question for me was Micah's personal condition the night of the wreck. Sheriff Franklin was certain Micah was on drugs the night of his wreck, but the autopsy suggested a different view. All of these questions remained a mystery to me which led to Forensic Science who did the full autopsy.

I put my trip off a year before I was ready to go to Forensic Sciences. I called and made an appointment to review the whole file. Earlier in the year, we had to get a Forensic Science report for a small insurance claim. This was the first time we saw a detailed report and cause of death on paper, which was a broken neck—Micah died instantly. There was some disturbing information on this report that puzzled me, Micah was clear from any drugs, but he did show .06 percent alcohol content in his blood stream. This bothered me greatly for a year until I went to visit the files and the attending doctor gave me an explanation. He said, "Forgive me but your son had seriously began discomposure; the alcohol content was right on target from the fermentation of a decomposing body." He said, "Mr. Giles, your son was clean the night of the wreck." That news set me free; Micah had a colorful past from age thirteen through sixteen. He stumbled along the way, but I was certain he was on the straight and narrow, particularly at his death. The hurtful notion for me was to have growing, whispering speculation by others of what caused his death. This trip to Forensic Science and the autopsy report put all of that to rest. The doctor there knew he gave me revelatory news. Micah was indeed clean. As his father, this was a huge burden off my chest.

Although the forensic report for some might be 180 degrees from our report, I urge you to refrain from the "what if" club. It is devastating and will hold you captive for years. Believe me, we have seen people clutched for a decade with guilt and pain by the death of a child. All of us can do better as parents, but when God blew his breath into Adam, he made him a living soul. Soul in scripture means mind, will, and emotions. As parents our goal is to raise healthy children who live productive lives contributing to fellow man and to society. It is never the wish of a parent for a child to be a liability and ultimately pay the big price for their mistakes and weaknesses. As Deborah so eloquently has spoken throughout this book, it is our perspective on death that determines the ability for God's grace to heal. If your child made wrong decisions that resulted in death, remember that God made them a living soul. Remember, Micah said it was his fault not our fault as parents for his misguided tours.

We all believe in personal responsibility, but your will cannot be superimposed onto your children's will. They have their own mind, will, and emotions. Their decisions can be most disappointing to us, and there is no kind of heartache like the heartache from a child making wrong decisions. Jesus said he came to heal the broken hearted. Let Him heal you from the pain of your child or loved one who made a wrong choice. He is the Great Physician. He healed the woman with the issue of blood with only the stroke of his garment touching her. My prayer, as you read this chapter on forensic science reports, is that you allow the Great Physician's garment to graze over you with the healing of this broken heart. Nothing else will heal this broken heart except a touch from almighty God. The reality comes when we sort out those concerns we can impact versus those concerns we cannot impact. It is impossible to return flushed water, so what is left in your hands, you can shape and mold. Let the Great Physician heal you today from the heartache that will not go away. You cannot outrun the heartache. Let him brush his garment over your wounded heart.

My first review was the photo file at the forensic science lab. Micah was recognizable but he had been through some serious blows to the body. His chest was greatly bruised from the steering wheel and his head had a nasty wound from the rear view mirror. His most recognizable features to me were his legs. As a father, you know your boys pretty well. The doctor was patient with me as I wanted to stare at the photo with his legs in full view.

Next was the video. They had to confirm his neck was broken, and the video footage I saw clearly confirmed his neck was broken on impact which caused his instant death. Although this visit, against my wife's strong recommendation, was grotesque at best, it certainly closed many loop holes for me. The autopsy report confirmed every detail of his death except why and how he left the road. Was it accidental? Was he trying to spare someone else's life? Or was he forced off the road? We may never know, and it is not going to change our perception of his death and our commitment to surrender to God's sovereignty. On one hand, I felt robbed by what would seem a premature death of my son; on the other, I felt such peace and comfort. As we have stated in this book many times, the scriptures teach us that life is indeed a vapor.

Micah always appeared to be one who was invincible and unconquerable. Witnessing him lying on that cold, stainless steel table, naked and lifeless, reminded me once again that human life is a gift from God. Life is priceless and no amount of money or treasures accumulated could or would be able to return Micah to me.

Although we have said goodbye to him for now, we will indeed meet again one day. It will not be for a season or for a lifetime of seventy years, but it will last forever and ever and ever.

Shucking Corn

By JOHN W. GILES

The reason I named this chapter "Shucking Corn" is because this gets down to where the rubber meets the road. Shucking Corn is an old southern metaphor used to describe peeling back all of the layers and getting down to the core of an issue. This chapter is devoted to expanding a little on the nuggets sprinkled throughout the book.

We have all heard the cliché that we are sometimes so heavenly minded we are no earthly good. It would be a fairly accurate assessment to deduce that when it comes to dealing with death; most become earthly minded and no heavenly good. We somehow can find ourselves trapped and imprisoned by our perspective. The master plan all along was for man- kind to live on earth for a season, make a difference with their life, and spend eternity in heaven. This was God's design from the Garden of Eden. Life on earth is temporal, life in heaven is eternal.

In a sense, life is much like preparing for a vacation. If our goal was to ultimately end up in the mountains on a ski trip, we would pack accordingly. If we pack bathing suits, sun- tan oil, umbrellas, and sand toys and we are going to the mountains skiing, we are going to be disappointed.

At the Santa Maria della Concezione dei Cappuccini church in Rome (better known as the bone church), some of the walls are lined with bones from monks who served there. While this is a bit odd to have bones on the walls, the message is clear; "As You Are, We Once Were...As We Are, So Will You Be." It is a sobering message that we need to think of our mortality when we attend a funeral or walk through the valley of the shadow of death ourselves. In Jewish customs, the first seven days after the death of a loved one is referred to as the Sheva. It is a time where we reflect on the person's life and on our own mortality as well. All of us who have attended a funeral think about death because we come face to face with it during the funeral. It is our opportunity, when attending a funeral, to take inventory of how we have packed. So the question is, how are you going to pack your bags?

If we go through life's journey preparing ourselves for heaven and eternity, then when death occurs, we should in a perfect world think eternity not earthly. The entire tone of this book is designed to help us see that when death or loss occurs, we need to shape our eternal perspective; not an earthly temporal perspective. We need to be ready for the slopes not the beach.

Titanium

Life is full of hardships and difficult days. All of us have our dark hours and days, some more than others, but we all have them. Losing a child was the most difficult trial of my life to date. I cannot imagine anything more challenging to face than this. But, if anyone knows what it is like to walk though the valley of the shadow of death, you can relate to this journey. In fact, it is almost a guarantee like Deborah told Micah's girlfriend, "there is nothing in life you cannot handle because this is as worse as it gets."

Somehow, some way God gives us special grace and unique anointing for these trials. All we have to do is be open and try to see His hand on our shoulder. It is true there is no substitute for experience. When one walks through a dark valley in life, it deepens his stride. It is like you walk just like your neighbor walks, but this experience gives substance and depth to your cadence.

We have all heard or read stories or watch movies where soldiers are taken captive as prisoners of war and tortured. They have been through and survived a horrendous chapter in their life. There is pain and pictures in their mind they wish would disappear. One thing is for certain, a soldier or civilian who survives the torture and abuse because they are citizens of, let's say, the United States of America, suddenly values their freedom more because being held in captivity against their will drives home the gift of freedom. There is a very high price paid for everyday to keep us free as a democracy. That person can without equivocation testify firsthand the cherished cost of freedom and in the same breath espouse in great detail the gift of being free once they are liberated. Friend, they can tell you about how wonderful and privileged it is to be free. These people walk with a new depth to their stride because of this experience.

Suffering is never the classroom of choice. We'd rather choose the easy classes and sail through to get our diploma in life without any scars associated with this degree. Those who have walked through and survived the valley of the shadow of darkness understand all too well the description mentioned about the depth and rhythm of their cadence. Often a term I find myself using associated with suffering is *titanium*. It's like we have titanium poured into our bone marrow. Suffering and going through the dark valley of the shadow of death gives one a different infrastructure tempered by the refining fire. The creditability one gains on the subject at hand unquestionably empowers them to speak with unmistakable authority. Through this experience, one indeed inherits an infrastructure of tempered titanium and walks with a much deeper stride with an unchallengeable cadence of this authority. Again, there is no substitute for experience. Anyone who has paid the price of suffering walks in this new cadence and their infrastructure is titanium filled.

What to Say, What to Do?

The awkwardness in approaching a friend, associate, or loved one who has suffered a loss is common place; everyone finds it very uncomfortable. You do not want to say anything that hurts but to the contrary you want to bring healing. It is always an awkward position we find ourselves in and no one is relaxed in this environment. It is not unique to feel weird or uncomfortable because everyone has these same conventional feelings.

It is always a bit difficult when our friends or those visiting feel the need to have something profound to say. Often it comes across as shallow and empty rather than authentic. Many times people mean well, but their answers are often pat or trite in nature. We have all probably been guilty of struggling at times to be profound or reaching deep for some revelation to share with someone in pain or need, but often we fail to ring the bell. With all due respect, some of our Christian friends sometimes want to come off spiritual and quote a "fix-it scripture," as if they just came off the mountain with Moses with the word for the hour. Listen, everyone really means well, but just relax, be yourself and measure your words. The bottom line is their words often come out of their mouth and fall flat to the ground producing little or no fruit or hurt.

On the other hand, they feel your unconditional love, and it produces a bountiful harvest.

When you experience a great loss in life, it is hard to verbalize what you need from those who love you. I can recall talking to people who suffered a loss and a common thread of discontentment was if they heard one more person say, "My thoughts and prayers are with you," they thought they would scream. Stay with me as I share a few practical suggestions in what to say and what to do.

Be there! Don't avoid those suffering loss because you feel awkward. Go see them at their house. Is it stiff, yes, but your presence and your warm, compassionate face speaks volumes. Be sure to sign the guest book because it will be a lasting memory that you shouldered the loss with them. If you only have thirty seconds one-on-one with those suffering, grab their hand, put your other hand on top of theirs, look them compassionately in the eyes, and tell them you are sorry and you love them. That is all you need to do. Your warmth, sincerity, and your eyes do the rest of the talking.

If you have more than thirty seconds, come prepared to share one quality, attribute, or something comical or quirky about the deceased. The loved ones are starving to hear something special about the departed loved one or how your life has been changed by the deceased. Talk about their good qualities or share some comical story. You will find yourself watering a thirsty soul.

Please try to refrain from saying; "If I can do anything, please call." While this may be a sincere overture, most people will not call on you. One suggestion is to talk to other close friends of the family or someone one or two tiers out from the immediate family and try to find a practical way to help. The fondest of our memories are those reaching out to us who found a niche to love on us and helped in a practical, common-sense way. We forgot all of those who said, "call me."

While on this subject of what to say, just know you can expect some of Job's friends to show up and pontificate a little. We all remember the biblical account where Job lost everything and he remained faithful to God. Others tried to undermine his faith and commitment to God raising all kinds of questions of doubt. We even had one person who was well meaning say we should have been tuned into the Holy Spirit a little closer so we could have prayed away Micah's death. You may find that hard to believe, but what they in essence were saying, is that if they had been in our situation they would have been so tuned into the Holy Spirit it would not have happened to them. How does this sound for edification to someone who just lost a child? We overlooked their overconfidence and forgave them but you can expect Job's friends to show up.

Hidden Treasures
Refrain from the "Why" and "What If" Questions

You may recall Deborah's challenge to me when we were on our way to the wreck site after the Sheriff called. As a reminder, she said this, "Let's make each other a promise to never say 'what if'." Not only has it helped us, but I share this all the time with those who have suffered a loss. While we all go through some varying levels of grief, opening the door to the "Why" and "What If" questions is a guaranteed journey to self pity. Life's trials can make you better or bitter.

It is also a guarantee if you swing open these doors you focus on who is missing rather than who is left behind.

Keep Them Alive In Your Heart

We will always remember the anniversary of Micah's death. This of course will be a difficult day to get through for the first few years. Many of your friends will remember and call you on this day to tell you they are praying for you on that landmark day. That is always nice when others remember your sorrowful day and help you shoulder the burden.

We have made it a practice until this day to have a family gathering on Micah's birthday. We will do this close to his birthday if not on his birthday of June twelfth every year. It is a wonderful time to get together and laugh about things he did or said. Micah, in nineteen years, gave us all plenty of fodder to ponder in his absence.

The Bible promises no more tears in heaven. So whatever happened causing the death, pain, and sorrow, it all evaporates in heaven. God is indeed perfectly just. Mourn and then get back as quickly as possible in celebrating life.

Give Thanks

During the holidays like Thanksgiving and Christmas, it is well advised to be grateful to God for the years you had with the loved one you lost rather than dwelling on their untimely departure and getting waste deep in grief and self pity from them being gone. It is an easy course of action to neglect those left behind while we swing wide open this door; it is very destructive to you and others. Try and envision it like a door you can close and lock shut. Although it seems impossible at the time, life can be fun once again.

The length of mourning is different for each person. Some may need to complement their journey with professional help. You can trust those who love you to tell you the truth. "Faithful are the wounds of a friend," (Proverbs 27:6). No one needs to tell you if you are slipping away; everyone knows in their heart the emotional and mental state of your being. Sometimes we may not want to face the truth and that is where we can really trust those who love us the most to speak the truth. Try not to shut them out; reach deep and be open to the truth spoken here in Proverbs. If they love you they will speak the truth to you even if the truth is painful. They love you and want you whole again.

We heard it more often than not that you will never get over losing a child. You are not showing any less love for or disrespect to your lost loved one if you have a normal, good day. In fact, you can have a normal healthy life after losing a child or loved one. Nothing in life should hold us captive or imprisoned. It is trust we looked forward to the day of reunion for this is biblically promised to us. There is a distinct difference between never getting over the loss of your child and looking forward to a reunion. One is temporal and one is eternal; only we can make that choice as to which path to follow.

Looking for Divine Signs and Fingerprints

In Part II of the book "Love Notes about Micah – Excerpts from Notes and Letters," we talk a lot about dreams and visions people had about Micah. In this chapter it is our wishes and intent to invoke hope.

"Now faith is the substance of things hoped for, the evidence of things not seen" (Hebrews 11:1). When you get down to it; hope is what carries us though each day after losing a loved one. It is pretty clear in this scripture that faith is substantiated by hope. Hope is the culprit for vision. Where there is no vision, the people perish, (Proverbs 28:19). If one wants to guarantee withering away, just remove hope. "And we know that all things work together for good to them that love God, to them who are the called according to his purpose" (Romans 8:28). These are not just trite scriptures being thrown out here, this is real. Hope says we will see you again one day, until we meet again. Along our journey to see them once again, we look for any little divine inspiration we can find to inspire hope that our loved ones are all right, which serves as fuel that we will indeed see them again.

People don't really die, they just change locations. It is healthy to think of your loved ones while they were here but also in eternity. They now have become a part of the great cloud of witnesses spoken about in Hebrews. That being said, it is only natural for us to look for divine signs and fingerprints.

Life is indeed a vapor, temporal at best. Death is so final once the earthly journey has concluded, yet from the perspective of eternity life goes on and on. No more two way conversations, no more feedback, no more hugs and the phone will never ring again with their voice greeting you on the other end of the phone line. That is it as far as earthly contact with the deceased. Sometimes as we find ourselves in denial we somehow expect the deceased loved one to walk back in the door. Eternity on the other hand is forever. Those left behind from the deceased grapple for any sign, symbol or any form of communication that the loved one is doing alright, in a better place or some manifestation of a visit. Your senses are on high alert for any sign or fingerprint of your loved one anywhere and in anyplace. You will find yourself watching butterflies, dragon flies, music, the sun breaking through clouds, wind, movies, sermons or discovered artifacts trying to speak to us a message of hope and comfort. We want to know they are doing alright and if they are trying to send us a message we do not want to overlook anything. You know, God spoke through a donkey so he can certainly use a butterfly to bring tranquility.

Peaking Into Heavens Window

It is our conclusion after losing a son that dreams and visions are given to loved ones and friends for a purpose. It has a way of allowing us to peak into heaven's window, which invokes hope and lets us see things from a different view.

One of the landmark visions we learned about was Stephen's vision of his brother the Monday afternoon we found Micah. Stephen saw his brother sitting at a white grand piano and he was wearing a white tuxedo with the tail draper over the piano bench. His brother loved playing the piano and singing. Micah, in this vision, looked up and made eye contact with Stephen and smiled. That one picture of his brother smiling communicated to Stephen that Micah was happy and at peace with his new situation. It was as though that snapshot froze, framed in Stephen's mind for weeks. As I mentioned during the visitation at Heritage Funeral Home, when I would break down emotionally, Stephen's big ole bear hand would rest on my shoulder, he would look me square in the eyes, and with all of the passion inside of him he would tell me, "Dad, Micah is okay; he is happy." God in His loving and redeeming way gave that vision to Stephen. It carried him through and this vision was used to help carry others through when Stephen would say it. I cannot tell you how many times that night he said it.

Deborah's sister Jennifer had a profound, life changing dream. She dreamed that Micah was calling her from a phone booth. In the dream, Micah was wearing white, the phone booth was white, and the phone was white. He told her, "Your vehicle is ready so you can get your kids and take them home. Don't be late. Come get it *now*." The Lord woke her up with, "Micah is calling!" She said she couldn't remember much. "Write it down!" a knowing from beyond urged. As she began writing, she began remembering. At the time, she was overwhelmed by emotions, crying but not sad. She also asked the Lord why He allowed Micah to be stolen from among us by the devil. God said, "He was not stolen, he was called home." We can all draw at least two conclusions from her encounter. If Micah was called home and not stolen then that should be our perspective. Looking at the death as being called home is viewing it as eternal not temporal. The other conclusion was it was a wakeup call that we need to get our house in order; no man knows the day or the hour.

Several of the dreams pointed toward an eternal perspective and not an earthly temporal point of view. In Micah's girlfriend's (Mary Margaret) dream, Micah said to her, "I am so sorry this happened to you." It wasn't what happened to him it was what happened to her. This caused Mary Margaret to view this through the eyes of heaven. Micah's friend Katie had a dream. Micah assured her he was in a better place and explained to her how wonderful it was. This helped Katie see through the Window of Heaven as well.

We learn that dreams and visions can serve as confirmations. In every case where someone came forward with a dream they had regarding Micah, it invariably pointed to an eternal perspective, not a temporal view at all. Death has many faces. It can be the loss of a loved one, divorce, deployed military, loss of job or a business, and even the death of a vision. When death strikes and it will, try to peak into the window of heaven.

Visitations

BY DEBORAH GILES

*No man is a failure
who has friends.*

*—It's a
Wonderful Life*

That night when we arrived at the funeral home chapel, I could not believe all the flowers. By the time I had walked through and tried to see whom they had come from, the people began arriving. From 5:40 in the evening until after nine thirty, we received friends, acquaintances, and public officials. We were unable to visit with some of our family members that came in after the line formed; we were tied up for hours by the steady flow of people.

I felt an anointing on me to minister to them. They had come to minister to me, yet I had to minister to most of them. The fear on some of their faces still stands out in my mind today. I just wanted to embrace them and assure them that Micah was with the Lord. I was reminded of the woman with the issue of blood who touched the hem of Jesus's garment. His reply was, "Who touched me?" because he felt virtue leave him. I felt that my embraces were imparting life. When I looked up the word virtue in Greek, I saw that it meant miraculous power and strength. I don't know if I imparted power, but I know people were receiving strength.

As the people moved through, John and I both began to realize just how many people we touch while moving through this life. It was like the movie *It's a Wonderful Life.*

Person after person reminded us of an event or a word of encouragement that had somehow impacted their life. In this hour, we were challenged to touch more people and impact more lives.

Many people commented on the fact that they had been in turmoil on their way to the funeral home that night. They said that when they entered the chapel, they were enveloped by the peace of God. That is because we were at total peace that Micah was with the Lord. The Lord had literally comforted them with the comfort that He had given to us.

One of the most common comments of the evening was from mothers who said, "This is my greatest fear." Having now experienced it, I knew that I was overcoming the fear of death. I had felt for many years that I had no fear of death, but now my faith had been tested. Now I knew! The fear of death is not just a fear of your own death. We need not fear death, even the death of a loved one. Our loved one is where we all hope to be someday. "To be absent from the body is to be at home with the Lord" (I Corinthians 5:8). In talking to David, Zavie, Stephen, and Mary Margaret, we had all undergone a transformation in our thoughts about death. None of us seem to have any real fear of death. A friend of mine in the pro-life movement in Atlanta, Georgia, received a death threat as she was counseling in front of an abortion clinic. Her response was, "Are you threatening me with heaven?" A lot of the problems we have in this life are really a problem with our perspective.

That night, when we arrived home, I took a sedative. We had a long day coming up with the funeral, and I needed sleep. Before we went to bed, our son, Stephen, announced to the family that he had written a song about his brother. We asked him to play it on his guitar and sing it for us. We were amazed that he had been able to write such a beautiful tribute to his brother in one day. As he played, I knew that he must play it at the funeral.

A Celebration of Life

By DEBORAH GILES

So we who are many, are one body in Christ.

Romans 12:5

At around three o'clock on the morning of the funeral, I woke up with a song in my heart, and I was literally singing it. The song was "I Am the Bread of Life." I awoke to the chorus "and I will raise him up, I will raise him up, I will raise him up on the last day." I also had a vision of Micah's coffin with incense coming up around it. The only way to describe how I felt that morning as I woke up was internally I was exploding with inspiration. I felt God's word was erupting like a volcano inside me.

I had to get up. I had a lot of work to do. This was Micah's big day. I also had a scripture on my heart: "Unless a grain of wheat fall to the ground and die, it abides alone, but if it dies it will bear much fruit." I knew He could even raise Micah from the dead if *He* chose to do so. I also knew then that I had the faith to see Micah raised from the dead, but I would rather see God's multiplying work take place. I believe that some of the fruit included those young men chosen to be pallbearers. There was a prayer in my heart to pray over them before the funeral.

John got up early and joined me as we sought the Lord for the direction of the funeral. We hammered out a program and finalized the details of the service. John's friend Hal Richardson with Minuteman Press that morning quickly produced, printed, and delivered the programs to the church in time for the funeral. Without much thought, I selected a white dress that I often wear on Easter or Mother's Day. My sister's husband Tim commented that my dress said it all.

Our friends had prepared a dinner at the church for our family and those participating in the funeral. Before we went down to the service, I requested that we gather the pallbearers, and I prayed what was on my heart. My prayer was that they would receive Micah's mantle of zeal for evangelism and that God would deliver them from weaknesses of the flesh.

The service started with Stephen singing the tribute he had written to his brother. At this time, John and I draped Micah's coffin with the Pall. It was a white linen cloth with the cross sewn into it. This signified Micah being covered in death by the cross of Christ. One of our friends commented that it was like John and I were tucking Micah into bed. We had several ministers read the Bible. The minister who dedicated and baptized Micah, John Varner, and a youth minister who was a friend to Micah provided eulogies. He shared about Micah's restaurant ministry. Then Terry Veazey, an evangelist from Montgomery, sang "God and God Alone" at which time the congregation rose to their feet to worship God. Terry and his wife had lost their first child in a drowning accident when he was only four. His name was also Micah and would have been our Micah's age.

All of the ministers who participated were in some way a part of our lives. Pastor John Varner was at the hospital the night Micah was born. He dedicated and baptized him. Pastor Steve Vickers was Micah's pastor through adolescence. Evangelist Mac Gober is a close personal friend of John's. When John left the family manufacturing business, he helped Mac in his ministry for six months. Pastor Mike Rippy is the pastor of our daughter and son-in-law. Our family frequently attends there and Micah loved their services. Pastor Claude Schufford pastors a neighborhood church that we had frequently attended. Father Jim Pinto, a charismatic Episcopal priest from Birmingham, who was our pastor and mentor at that time, officiated over the service. It seems that he was there for us for every major event in our lives. When I began my pro-life ministry, Jim was there to help. When Micah went off to military school, Jim just happened to call us that day to pray for us. He baptized Stephen and our granddaughter, and he did pre-marriage counseling and conducted the wedding for Zavie and David.

The service closed with the serving of Holy Communion. Communion is very important to our family. Some of our most special times as a family were as we partook of communion in our living room during a midday prayer time. So John and I were honored when Father Pinto asked us to present the elements of communion. We carried the wine and bread up to the front of the church.

My feelings about participating in the funeral were very odd to me. Almost two years earlier, when our daughter married, I did not want to assume the traditional active role in the execution of the wedding as the bride's mother. What I wanted was to be escorted to my seat and be removed from the center stage of the action. I am by nature a back stage person anyway. My son Micah escorted me to my pew; he was the perfect handsome gentleman.

Communion was such a vital component in Micah's walk with God. I remember one time when Micah got in trouble with an accountability group he was a part of because he used real wine when he served communion to them. He didn't see any problem with it, but as you can imagine, this caused quite a stir in an Assembly of God church.

The priest who served the communion at Micah's funeral thought at one point that he might have to ask the Lord to multiply the loaves and the fishes because almost everyone present came forward to receive. The most common comment that we have heard about this service was that the people felt they had experienced the coming together of the whole body of Christ. This was mainly due to so many denominations being represented by the clergy and the variety of expressions incorporated into the service.

The morning of the funeral, I awakened and saw Micah's coffin with incense coming up around it. At the end of the service, the priest put incense around Micah's coffin. The Word states that the Lord will bless the nations that burn incense to Him. The incense also signifies the prayers of His people coming up before His throne. I believe that Micah's service was a sweet smelling aroma as the body of Christ came together as one. We had a communion of the saints in heaven and on earth.

Micah and Mary Margaret

Life Celebration Service
for

Micah Worthington Giles
June 12, 1979 - May 15, 1999

at

Frazer Memorial United Methodist Church
Montgomery, AL

May 20, 1999

One o'clock p.m.

*And Jesus answered them, saying, "The hour has come for the Son of Man to be glorified. **Truly, truly, I say to you, unless a grain of wheat falls into the earth and dies, it remains by itself alone; but if it dies, it bears much fruit.** He who loves his life loses it; and he who hates his life in this world shall keep it to life eternal. If anyone serves Me, let him follow Me; and where I am, there shall My servant also be; if anyone serves Me, the Father will honor him."*
(John 12:23-26)

Father Jim Pinto

Celebrants

Rev. Rick Blackerby Rev. Michael Rippy
Rev. Mac Gober Rev. Claude Shufford
Rev. Lamar Golden Rev. John Varner
Rev. Steve Vickers

Pall Bearers

Joseph Byrom Joseph Jennings
Friend Friend
Jeremy Cartright John Lefere
Friend Cousin
Will Frye Jeremiah Merritt
Friend Friend
William O. Giles, III Griffin Petranka
Cousin Mary Margaret's Brother

The Committal at Graveside

Alabama Heritage Cemetery

Comments and Prayer - Reverend Mac Gober

Psalm 23 - Reverend Claude Shufford

"Amazing Grace" - Reverend Terry Veazey

Committal - Father Jim Pinto

The Lord's Prayer

A special thank you to all of you who have been by our side all these past few days. Your untiring vigil with prayers, your presence and service to our family will never be forgotten.

Worship Music Concert
Julie Roy

A Tribute to My Brother
Stephen Giles

*Processional

Opening Prayer
Reverend Claude Shufford

Old Testament Reading
Reverend Michael Rippy

Psalm
Reverend Lamar Golden

The Epistle Reading
Reverend Steven Vickers

*The Gospel Reading
Father Jim Pinto

"Be Thou My Vision"
Dottie James Parker
Flute Accompanist
Betsy James

Eulogies
Reverend John Varner Reverend Rick Blackerby

"God, and God Alone"
Reverend Terry Veazey

Holy Eucharist - Communion
Father Jim Pinto

Communion for all believers

The Commendation

The Blessing

Dismissal

*Recessional

*Please stand

The family of Micah Giles thanks you for all your kindness,
prayers and love. It is our desire that these excerpts from
a paper he wrote earlier this year be shared with you at
this service of thanksgiving for his life.

"The first major step in becoming a Christian is
admitting that you are a sinner in need of a
Savior. In order to do this, one must understand
first that 'all have sinned and fall short of
the glory of God.'

The second major step to becoming a Christian
is putting one's faith in Jesus to save one from
his sins. All God expects of us is to have 'faith
as the grain of a mustard seed.'

The process of putting one's faint in Jesus is
done by a simple prayer spoken in faith, for the
Bible states that 'if you confess with your mouth
and believe with your heart that Jesus Christ is
Lord then you shall be saved.'

God has given man direct access to Him through
prayer. In the same way that a person cannot
have a relationship with another without
speaking, neither can we have relationship
with God without conversation with Him through prayer.

In summary, through repentance, the reading of
God's word, and prayer, one can live this
life as a Christian."

Written by
Micah W. Giles
1999

A complete copy of these papers are provided as you exit the church for
your edification and is a gift from this child of God to the people of God.

A CELEBRATION O

It seemed as though it was taking forever to get the funeral program on paper. John is such an organized person, and it seemed as though he was having great difficulty focusing on this task that had to be completed. Caroline his sister was a lifesaver. She helped us get it all finalized, and she wrote the obituary for us. John still remembers how the peace mentioned earlier can sometimes take you into a stunned or numbed state somehow, by God's grace and mercy, cushioning the impact.

Closer Than We Think

By DEBORAH GILES

Therefore, since we have so great a cloud of witnesses surrounding us,...

Hebrews 12:1

The next day after the funeral, the family wanted to go out to the cemetery. My sister in-law, Caroline, and I removed all the flowers from the various arrangements to fashion some dried arrangements for the family. After this, John wanted to go to the wreck site and place a marker.

When we got there, John and my brother in-law went down the embankment to the place where the Jeep came to rest. While they were gone, it was hot, so I got back in the car and a Don Moen worship tape was playing, "...I just want to be where you are; dwelling daily in your presence, I don't want to worship from afar; draw me near to where you are..." As I began to enter into worship, I felt profound assurances that Micah was with Him and that when I entered into worship, I was not only near Jesus, I was also near Micah. This was the beginning of my new inspiration on the communion of the saints who have passed from death into life. We can enter into the life of God from this side of heaven, but we see dimly, as in a glass mirror. The place we are here is temporal; over there it is eternal.

For many years, I had viewed the church differently than most of body. I believe when looks at the city of Montgomery, he only sees one church. He does not see the broken body that we have created. He sees us together in unity and harmony. "This is how the world will know that we are His disciples because we love one another" (John 13: 34-35). It has always been my desire as a Christian for the body of Christ to be one and not segmented. When the church catches the vision that when one segment of the body prospers or is healthy the whole body benefits, then we will begin nourishing and blessing all of the parts of the body of Christ. We are not in competition with one another.

Now, the Lord was beginning to break open to me new understanding that the body here on earth is one with the body in heaven. Whether we see it or not, God's church in heaven and earth are one. The church militant on earth is fighting the good fight and the church triumphant in heaven is cheering us onward. Just as the book of Hebrews refers to "the great cloud of witnesses," these saints surround us (Hebrews 12:1).

When the men came up the hill from the wreck site, we gathered in a circle to pray. Delano, our brother in-law, prayed about this spot where Micah exited this life. It was one of the many ironies that it was here, in this place, that God allowed Micah to make his own final exit off the highway of this life. It was Micah's final exit off I-65.

Later that day, I was alone at home, and I began the task of putting my home back in order. The funeral home van arrived with all the potted plants that had been sent to us. As they began unloading, I thought about how the plants could be seen as a lifetime of Mother's Day and Christmas gifts from my son. I was full of the joy of the Lord, and I marveled at the fact that "my cup runs over" (Psalms 23:5). In my mind, all I could think was that this was not natural. I shouldn't feel like this. I asked myself some questions, "Shouldn't I be sad and mourning? Is it wrong for me to be happy because I just buried my son? My feelings here were not normal; am I in denial or is God helping me to see all of this through His eyes?"

On Friday, we retrieved Micah's pickup truck from the shop where it was being repaired. It contained eight Gideon New Testaments and a stack of gospel tracts. The Bibles were given to Micah's pallbearers, and my son in-law cleaned up the truck so we could give it to Joey, Micah's best friend.

Sunday, we wanted to attend several churches because so many congregations in Montgomery had embraced us. If there had been time in that day, I am sure we would have attended more services.

Later that day, we gave Joey Micah's truck and that was the last time we saw him for months. Joey was struggling with the loss of his friend, Micah, and it was obvious he was entering into a spiritual desert. All of us as Christians know we all go through those spiritual deserts, but that usually is where we find God. Joey's father died when he was a teen, and Micah was the closest male in his life.

Monday was a day of new beginnings for our family. Our granddaughter who was due the day Micah's body was found was born. This birth came to the minute one week after Micah was found. They named her Grace. I couldn't have said it better myself. If ever we had a picture of God's grace, this was it. Her birth and her name are an unfolding of grace to us. She was also a picture that life does indeed go on. "The Lord gave and the Lord has taken away. Blessed be the name of the Lord" (Job 1:21).

Dreams and Visions

BY DEBORAH GILES

*Then God said to
him in a dream…*

Genesis 20:6

Almost immediately after Micah's death we began hearing stories of dreams and visions that friends and relatives had received concerning Micah. These stories served to encourage the fainthearted and in some cases brought others back to their spiritual roots with Christ. As I was writing this, I received a phone call from an old friend who shared with me a near death experience she had years ago while suffering with a deadly heart problem. Her spirit left her body at one point. She said she did not cross The River but will never forget the heavenly music that she heard. She said she saw Jesus, and He asked if she wanted to stay. She told me that she foolishly asked to go back to see her grandchildren grow up. She believes that the Lord must still have something for her to do or he would have already taken her home.

As I shared earlier, John's father, W.O., had a dream before he died. In this dream, W.O. and Micah were in a large coliseum. W.O. said the crowd was very unruly and noisy. When he came out, he introduced Micah as the next John-the Baptist. Then Micah appeared on the stage in a white robe and as he reached the position to speak, he jerked his arm and the place became totally silent. This somehow seems like a foretelling of Micah's ministry beginning after his death.

The first dream after Micah's death that I recall was Stephen's. Stephen said in the dream he questioned Micah with, "I thought you were dead?" Micah said that he thought he was dead but had no memory of the event. He also told Stephen that he liked what the family had decided to do for a marker on his grave.

Two weeks after Gracie was born, we took the family to Destin for a much-needed vacation at the beach. We invited Mary Margaret who was to join us mid-week. When she arrived, she was full of life. She had seen Micah in a dream the night before. In the dream, she and I were sitting on a bed talking. I was telling her about all the times that Micah had left home. Then Micah appeared in the room, but she said it wasn't like she needed to run to him. He asked her, "When did this happen to you?" referring to his death. She told him she was nineteen when it happened. He responded with genuine sorrow at her misfortune, "I am so sorry this happened to you." It was as if nothing had happened to him, it had only happened to us.

A common thread that ran through these visitations with eternity was the fact that there is no concept of time on the other side. A thousand years is like one day and one day is as a thousand years (2 Peter 3:8). This seemed to be a glimpse into one of the mysteries of heaven. After Micah's death, I lost interest in wearing a watch. I found this strange because I too was beginning to get a heavenly glimpse of timelessness.

A month or so later Jennifer, my sister, had a dream that would literally restore her relationship with Christ. She dreamed that Micah was calling her from a phone booth. In the dream, Micah was wearing white, the phone booth was white, and the phone was white. He told her, "Your vehicle is ready so you can get your kids and take them home. Don't be late. Come get it *now*." The Lord woke her up with, "Micah is calling!" She said she couldn't remember much. "Write it down!" a knowing from beyond urged. As she began writing, she began remembering. At the time, she was overwhelmed by emotions, crying but not sad.

She asked the Lord why had she had a Micah dream? She was told that she had had one before but she did not write it down. It was gone. Then the Lord revealed to her that the witness that Micah bore for God in life is continued in his death. She remembered Micah talking to her on our front porch one day about the importance of accepting Jesus as Savior and *living* for Him. Then she knew why she had received the dreams. She had accepted Jesus as Savior but knew that she was not living her life as an example of truth to other people.

She said Micah wants us to write down these dreams so that we can continue in his witness for God. We can become strong examples and witnesses in everything that we do. He wants us to share what we know as he shared what he knew and saw. The Word exhorts us in Acts 4:20: "We cannot stop speaking about what we have seen and heard." In Micah's life, he reached out to others about the importance of putting God first and keeping Him there, and his death became a startling reality. What are we doing for Christ today? What does our witness say to those who are in contact with us? If we die today, will most people know we had a life changing experience with Christ?

She asked the Lord why he allowed Micah to be stolen from among us by the devil. God said, "He was not stolen, he was called home." She recalled the scripture; "Those who have insight will shine brightly like the brightness of the expanse of heaven, and those who *lead* many to righteousness, like the *stars forever and ever!*" (Daniel 12:3). The Lord was going to teach us all a great lesson about trust. God did not make a mistake. There is so much that we cannot comprehend in God's vastness, but our incomprehension does not change the reality or the purpose of those things.

The Lord showed her that Micah understood the importance of reaching out in love. She could see all the lives he had touched, and is touching. Men who live to be 120 may never touch so many. It is not just the lost, but also those who have grown cold who need to renew their love and enthusiasm for the Lord. Those Micah impacted are like a snowball rolling down a snowy hill. They can gather mass (continue in *love*) and have a great impact for Jesus.

She remembered how the witness of a hitchhiker that she never saw was instrumental in bringing her to Christ. She said that a friend who had picked the hitchhiker up was commenting on what this hitchhiker had said about Jesus changing his life. My sister laughed and said she did not believe that God could change someone's life. To this her friend said, "He did." She immediately felt convicted and sorry for what she had said. She even remembers thinking, "I don't even believe what I just said." Those words were used to bring her to a conversion within a few short months. They were the words of a hitchhiker that she had never seen.

Micah's friend, Katie, had a dream in which Micah was again calling on a telephone:

I had this dream that Micah called me from heaven. We had a nice conversation, but I told him that I missed him. As I cried to him, I kept asking him why God had to take him away so soon. I told him that I never got to say good-bye to him or tell him how much he meant to me. I told him that he was like a big brother to me. Micah assured me that he was in a much better place. He told me how wonderful it was. I kept asking him why? We continued talking, and I cried to him, and he told me not to worry, that he would be here soon to take me back with him. And then I woke up.

My daughter Zavie's dream took place the night before a planned "Micah party" that our friends Tom and Jan Kotouc had organized. The Kotouc's invited some of our dearest and close friends over to their house for a "Micah Party," which was designed to glean back over the positive qualities of Micah's life. In the dream, Zavie was at the party and the main meeting had broken up after which the people were dispersing throughout the house in fellowship. She was in the hall, and her eye focused on a particular group. As she looked closer, one of the people was Micah. She said he was dressed up very nice in a dress shirt and a tie. She said it was as if no one else seemed to see him. She ran over and hugged him tightly and kept saying, "I love you." He said, "I love you, but don't worry, I'm coming back with Jehovah Rophi." The hug was comforting, and she felt secure in his arms. She didn't remember letting go, but as she started to turn around he was gone.

She said that ever since he died, she wished she could hug him one more time. She even wished she could remember the last time she hugged him and what it felt like. When she looked up the name Jehovah Rophi, she discovered that it means *Jehovah heals*. She said that hugging him that one last time healed her.

About a month after Micah's death, one of his preschool teachers dropped by the house to give us a tape from Brownsville Assembly of God. While we were visiting, she related a dream that she had just had. In the dream, Micah was sitting at a dining room table visiting with her. He told her what a good dad John had been to him. This message coming from a third party was very comforting for John.

The summer before Micah died, he and I were sitting in the living room talking (a favorite pastime for Micah). He told me that he believed that the Lord was telling him he was not going to marry or have children. I remember telling him that that would be a disappointment, but if that was God's will, I knew it would be good. After he died, Mary Margaret told us that he had told her he didn't believe they would marry because they would be separated by a car accident. Then he would be free to fully concentrate on ministry. She did not share his enthusiasm about the expanded ministry possibilities.

One of the keys I have found to unlocking the biblical meanings of events in our lives is an understanding of the use of numbers. There is a fear in the church about placing significance to the use of numbers. I certainly understand this because of the occult or new-age teaching of numerology. That being said, we do have to be cautious because the devil does on occasions try to create a counterfeit to God's authenticity. Numbers played a significant role in our understanding of what God was doing in our lives during this experience.

The following is a brief overview of a study on the significance of biblical numbers:

One — Used when marking the beginning of things, primacy, and unity

Two — Agreement, fellowship, union with Christ; two are a witness, difference, division, or a double portion

Three — The Trinity, or Triune Godhead, perfect witness; this number usually indicates something of importance or significance in God's plan of salvation by identifying an important event in salvation history. This number operates as a sign-post in Scripture study for the reader to pay attention to the significance of the next event. Jonah was in the belly of the whale for three days. Jesus arose on the third day. His parents left Jesus in Jerusalem three days.

Four — The number four represents God's creative works, especially works associated with the earth: Earth (four winds or four corners of the Earth). "The city was laid out like a square"(Revelations 21:16).

Five — Grace; five kinds of animals were sacrificed in the old covenant, Jesus had five wounds

Six	Both man and the serpent were created on the sixth day, therefore, the number six represents both man and rebellion
Seven	Perfection, completion (seven or seventh is used 549 times in the Bible)
Eight	It is the number of salvation, resurrection, and new birth/regeneration; new beginning (new world began with eight people, a new week is the eighth day)
Nine	Fruit of the Spirit, nine Beatitudes, it is self-repeating (nine multiplied by any number, then adding the numbers in the answer always ends in nine). Nine is also the number of finality or judgment
Ten	Responsibility on earth; completeness and perfection
Eleven	Human failure; confusion; judgment, disorder, also disorganization, unfulfillment, imperfection
Twelve	Number for earthly government (12 tribes; 12 Apostles)
Forty	Has an association both as a time of consecration and as a period of trial or testing; (Noah and Jesus in the desert)
Fifty	Year of Jubilee or deliverance

Micah died going off bridge number five between Millbrook and Montgomery. He was missing three days.

He had turned his life over to Christ and been converted for three years. He had been back home for three months after leaving home to live on his own in Arizona. He had been dating Mary Margaret for three years. Micah died in the fifth month of the year.

The Bible says we are to judge things by their fruits. The fruits of these visits were to comfort and steer people back onto the path of life. I believe they were the work of the Holy Spirit. He came to comfort and guide us.

Our Treasures

By DEBORAH GILES

*For where your
treasure is,
there will your
heart be also.*

Luke 12:34

The treasures that we stored up over our life will either make us or break us in the fiery trials of life. Jesus said to the Jews who believed in Him, "If you continue in My word, then you are truly disciples of Mine; and you will know the truth and the truth will make you free" (John 8:32). Many who call themselves Christians cannot qualify as disciples because they have not continued in His Word. Years ago, I heard the Bible teacher Marilyn Hickey say, "Can the Word." You must continually put up cans of the Word for the day that you will need it." I have seen many Christians crumble in times of crisis. They have no reservoir to draw from.

The Word is manna from heaven. It must be gathered daily and used. I can't imagine just eating a cracker a day. That's how some Christians live—one dry morsel a day for the spirit and three whopping feasts for the flesh. They don't believe in fasting physical food, but have no trouble fasting the Word of God. Jesus said, "Man shall not live by bread alone but by every word that proceeds from the mouth of God" (Matthew 4:4).

About five years ago, evangelist Flip Benham of Operation Rescue challenged me in this area. He asks people every time he speaks to read through the

Bible every year. The first year I didn't make it. It is a tremendous commitment. The next year I bought a Bible designed to be read-through in one year. It is arranged by the date and gives you about five chapters per day to read. I successfully read through the Bible for a consecutive four years. The only way for the Holy Spirit to bring the scriptures *to your remembrance* is for it to already be planted there.

I believe that there are many messages in these passages, but a key to me is the fact that the inspiration of God's Word is a rock that we can build on. When our Father reveals something to us by His Spirit, hell cannot take it from us. Learning the Word with our head is important, but until the Lord touches that Word and makes it alive to us, it is just words. It is like the wedding feast where Jesus performed his first miracle. He had them fill the pots with water. It was no coincidence that there were six vessels—six is the number of man. No one would have known it was wine unless it had been poured out and served (John 2:11). We take in the word, but until we begin pouring it back out to others, no one would ever know if what we had was water or wine. In a sense, Jesus transforms us from water into wine so we might be poured out on the lives of others. Wine is a typology of blood and we too can be used to be poured out as healing to others.

God wants His Word to become flesh and dwell among us. His Word is a light for our path and a lamp for our feet. I have watched many in the church struggle with "What am I supposed to be doing?" His Word is there to light the way. The reason many are lost is that they either have an empty vessel or they may have never used any of what they have. I am challenged by the words "to whom much is given much is required" (Luke 12:48). I know too much to not act on His revealed Word.

Grieve Not

By JOHN & DEBORAH GILES

Why is it that we rejoice at a birth and grieve at a funeral? It is because we are not the person involved.

—Samuel Clemens

Early in this experience of losing our son, 1 Thessalonians 4:13 spoke to me. "We do not want you to be uninformed, brethren, about those who are asleep (dead), so that you will not grieve as do the rest who have no hope." There are two components to grief. One is the fear of not knowing where your loved one is. The other is dealing with the separation of your loved one. To overcome these components you need faith in God's love and trust that there is a hereafter.

My husband and I had lost our fathers within a month of each other three years before Micah's death. Neither of us suffered any real grief. Part of this we believe is due in part to our having no unfinished business. We missed our fathers, but we knew that one day we would be reunited.

On his deathbed, John's father had an awesome experience with God. It was as though his vision was only on the next world. He was talking with us but his vision was centered in eternity. He spoke of seeing a lot of people from all over the world. He recognized a man that he had known in business, James Vineyard, who had passed on many years ago. He talked about a river, but at that point he was not allowed to cross.

He crossed that river several days later. My faith in the next life was already firm, but experiences like this one served to cement my beliefs. I read several books that studied life changes in people who had near-death experiences. A common thread in all of these people who had near-death experiences in their lives were dramatically impacted and changed for the better. Another thread was those with them in that experience sometimes benefited in the same way. I believe I am one of those people.

I personally do not think there is enough emphasis on what awaits us in the next life. If we could see what glories our loved ones are experiencing in heaven, we would never wish them back.

One Wednesday night shortly after Micah died, I had the thought that being in heaven and having loved ones on earth who will not let go is like being on the vacation of a lifetime and calling home only to have your family put a guilt trip on you or to have them beg you to come back. The Sunday after Micah died, before they found the Jeep, I kept having the thought, "Let him go." This was confirmed several days later when a friend, June Russell, who could not come to the funeral, wrote me a note. She said the Lord told her to tell us, "Let him go." I believe the same way June did, I needed to let him go which is very important in the healing process. We have to let them go. Not letting them go is in direct opposition to God's greater design.

I am by nature a very controlling person. Letting go of Micah is somewhat comforting to me. I know God is in control and I need to let go and let Him take me where He wills. As long as we hang onto things that are out of our control we are miserable. I know where my son is. I plan to join him someday. Until that day, I must fill my time with God's will for my own life.

One of the things that I do not understand about the grieving process is what happened to our friends who were far away. It seemed that they experienced tremendous turmoil. Those that were close I believe were comforted by the peace that God had given us. Three close friends who were far away and could not be with us had difficulty finding peace in this situation.

One of the counterfeits that I have found that masquerades as grief is actually self-pity. The days that I was emotionally very low were days that I allowed myself to indulge in self-pity. This is a very destructive course of action to fall into. The times that our family indulged in it, we had to fight to be released from it. I do not dwell on missing Micah. I miss him, but I try to keep it in perspective. When we meditate on the fact that "life is but a vapor" instead of how long we may be apart, we have hope, just as a runner in a race seeing where the finish line is can pace himself to finish the race. John had a real struggle with this eternity versus temporal question on Micah's would-be twentieth birthday. The following is an account by John in his own words.

> Every year it is an annual tradition for all of us to go to the beach in Destin, Florida, and stay at the former Silver Beach Motel and Cottages. We pack up everybody, including my daughter, her husband, Micah, his girlfriend, Mary Margaret, Stephen, and Deborah. It was always something the whole family looked forward to—a full week of doing nothing except sitting under an umbrella, enjoying a good book, meditating on the goodness of God, and feeling the gentle sea breeze and hearing the sound of

children playing in the gulf, not to mention our Friday night favorite, which was to visit the Hilton Hotel at San Destin where the chef always puts on one fabulous, all-you-can-eat, fresh seafood buffet.

I recall that day on the side of the interstate at the wreck site when we were waiting on them to positively indentify our son in the Jeep. I said to Deborah, "How can we go to the beach without Micah this year?" Deborah said, "We are going." For, you see, it was the seventeenth of May and we were going to the beach in about three weeks. Micah's birthday is June 12, and he would have been twenty years old.

On Saturday, June 12, 1999, everyone had returned home from the beach except Deborah and me. We saw the children off, and it got awfully quiet—too quiet. We were under the umbrella at the beach, and it was a bit overcast that morning, not your typical warm, Gulf day at the beach. It was a bit cool, and without any of the children around and the realization of it being Micah's birthday, it hit me square between the eyes: it was Micah's birthday, he is gone and I was lost without my boy. Where is my son? I did not buy him anything for his birthday. I could not talk to him that day, let alone hug him and tell him I love him. It was common place in the Giles house to say "I love you" several times a day.

I was not enjoying the beach anymore, and I became restless. Of course, when I said something to Deborah about how I was feeling, she gave me a spiritual answer, which I might add was from the Lord; Deborah is a very devoted, godly lady who feeds on God's word constantly. I just rejected it as some spiritual little antidote that is supposed to heal my sorrow. Well, I snapped back at her because I was not looking for a way out of this emotional downward spiral I was in. I just wanted to miss him for a while. This was very unproductive for I was setting myself up for self-pity and creating an environment for unnatural sorrow to set in and take charge. Well, I blew it and had Deborah mad at me for sparring back at her for her correct response to the situation. Now I was in the doghouse and had rejected her spiritual counsel, so we packed up prematurely and got on the road back to Montgomery. I might add there was not much conversation because I had bruised her with my barking. The Lord was dissatisfied with my reaction, but Satan, who we know is the accuser of the brethren was doing fine with my course of action.

What made it worse was we came through Luverne, Alabama, where we always ate fried chicken at the Chicken Shack. The Chicken Shack was a restaurant that served chicken prepared and cooked with our family recipe and in our specially-designed cooker. Our family business, had notoriety for the commercial chicken frying equipment and process better known as "Chester Fried Chicken." The Chicken Shack was one of the oldest establishments in the nation that served "Chester Fried Chicken." What made this stop worsen my woes is the boys and I were members of a hunting club in Crenshaw County and we would always come out of the woods and eat at the Chicken Shack. I was really missing Micah. The memory of eating fried chicken with Micah and Stephen at the Chicken Shack left me feeling hollow as if one of my major organs had been removed. I was also reminded sitting there that Micah had killed a six point buck just a few miles from there in the fall of 1998 before he was killed in the spring of 1999.

I think what began to heal me was reading the local newspaper I saw at the Chicken Shack. It had a headline story of a black youth who was killed in an automobile accident that weekend. Automatically, I wanted to find this young man's parents and minister to them. It was an instinct, much like a mission, where I had to find them and go see them.

Later, when I got home, I called the funeral home and got the information on how to contact the parents. I prayed and asked God to deliver me from this awful and destructive pain. I realized later that he sent me in front of the newsstand so I could begin to think of others rather than myself. I was able to talk with the boy's parents and followed up with a note. This act became a key to healing. As we reached out to others suffering loss, we were also healed in the process.

Of course, I apologized to Deborah for being very insensitive among other things. The bottom line is that I allowed myself to slip from missing my son to unnatural sorrow, to a grief-stricken state, to self-pity.

Throughout this journal you will hear about Deborah's inspiration from God about never saying "what if." I really believe this was an inspiration from God and will be a great help for many who will receive this counsel. I can tell you from experience, anyone who has lost a child or loved one from a tragic experience thinks about what they could have done to intervene and intercept the circumstances precluding their death. The bottom line is that God was not asleep at the switch when my son went off the interstate that night. Whenever one begins to drift to an area of interception, it should be a cue to kick into the "no 'what if' mode." Never say *what if*—save yourself a lifetime of pain. Just *do not go there*.

Another instance in my short stint with grief was when Deborah recognized that I might be drifting into a reclusive state; certainly this was not my mode of operation. It was Tuesday, May 25, 1999, Micah had been dead just over one week; We had buried him five days earlier, and we just saw the birth of our first grandbaby the day before on

Monday, May 24. I always go to work early, but as I drove in the parking lot behind my office, I parked and began walking down the sidewalk. I was serving as president for the Christian Coalition of Alabama. I can vividly recall that walk down the sidewalk as if it was yesterday. I remember saying to myself as if I was talking to someone else, "So I am supposed to go into this office, fight for what is right and against all evil, change the world by changing Alabama, and I am supposed to do this without my son? Yeah right." When I said the word son it was as though I was describing a major organ in my abdomen that had been ripped from inside me. This was a vital organ that I knew I could live without because I was walking, talking, and breathing, but I was still hemorrhaging deeply.

Later in the morning, I believe Deborah called, or I called her, and it was obvious to her that I was not hitting on all eight cylinders. I was a little short, curt, and desperately enjoying my privacy. I did not want to talk to anyone. I wanted some quiet. I am one who usually sorts out my troubles alone anyway or with my wife, who is my best friend in the whole world. I would have been content to be alone and to continue my sorting process, but Deborah thought differently. She was trying to think of someone I would respect and not brush off, but she had to work it quietly and have them show up. She called our friend, Pam Williams. who was the sister of Denise Vickers. Steve and Denise Vickers were our pastors for several years, and I have the deepest respect for them.

It was about two that afternoon, and I was paying some bills and balancing some checking accounts, which is depressing in itself without a major life crisis. The phone rang while my assistant was buzzing in and out of my office. In the midst of this activity, Pastor Steve Vickers walked by the window outside my office. I thought, *Where in the world is he going?* and then I heard the back door of our office simultaneously open—it was Pastor Vickers.

He came in and said "What's up, man?"

I said, "Not a whole lot,"

He said "Let's go."

I said "Okay, where are we going?"

"I don't know, but we are getting out of here."

Rarely do I have to depend on others for direction, but I must say I laughed at him, and I was glad to see him. I was ready to get out of there, and I wanted to go, just simply go with no direction or purpose—just go. He started driving due east, which was straight down Adams Avenue, which then turns into Mount Meigs Road, which then turns into the famous Atlanta Highway. He was pumping me for conversation, and I was easing into it gently.

When we were almost to the eastern bypass, he stopped the car, got out and said, "You drive!"

I asked him, "Where do you want me to drive?"

He said, "Wherever you want to go."

I knew I either wanted to go to the cemetery or the wreck site. I told him, "Let's go to the wreck site,"

He said, "Okay, here we go."

I took him to the site, and I walked him through, step-by-step, Micah's remaining minutes and seconds of his life. I relived that wreck, and oddly enough this did me a world of good. We then went to Burger King and had some coffee. I know how busy Pastor Vickers is, and he was devoting all of this concentrated personal time to me. I might add he was not providing me with any deep revelatory counsel, he was just being my friend, allowing me to talk about the wreck.

There are two lessons here. First, to those like myself who are in deep pain, it is not good to be alone during this time. Even when you think it is best or you can swim through this alone, that is when you need to find a friend and go for a ride or to the woods or whatever. Also, for the friend being the comforter, you do not need to be a great counselor seeking deep inspiration to shed light. You simply need to be yourself and be there. This day brought a great deal of healing. I was able to laugh, cry, and talk. I will always remember Pastor Steve Vickers's trip to my office. It brought healing to me when I was aching deeply; unless you have been there you cannot imagine how deep this ache can go. It seems as though there is no relief or escape from this type of heartache.

Some may ask the question, "How can I have fun when my loved one is dead?" You feel like you died too, and in some cases you feel guilty if you enjoy life and laugh. The word of God is so true, "A merry heart doeth good like a medicine" (Proverbs 17:22). Immediately, our family began to relive the joy, laughter, and inside jokes we all have enjoyed throughout the years. Micah was very humorous, and we laughed and cried as a family. This by no means was a state of denial of his death, but it served as godly therapy during those critical hours after his death and beyond. Our laughter about Micah and some of his uniqueness was not disrespectful, but it could be and should be viewed as giving honor and allowing God to soothe the pain through a joyful heart, even though there is great pain.

As his mother, maybe I am able to grasp this better because of how practical Micah was because he got this from me. He was a rolling party. Wherever he went there was fun and mischief. I know that he would not want me to mope around. He is cheering me on.

I have felt people pull away from us several times since Micah's death for fear that they did not know what to say. I can't speak for everyone who has suffered this sort of loss, but I enjoyed talking about my son. Those who expressed sorrow at our loss and told us we were in their thoughts touched us and allowed us to express our feelings. It is those who pretend that nothing has happened that bother me the most. This in some ways makes Micah's passing a non-event.

One thing that really ministered to all of us was for someone to recount a time or incident that they remembered about Micah. Those were precious and meaningful moments that we shared with our friends. These recorded accounts were very special because they took time to drop a note recounting those special memories.

I wish people wouldn't stay away because they feel inadequate to minister. We are all inadequate to do anything without Christ. We can tell you from personal experience that just the fact that you cared enough to come by ministered to us. One mental picture that I cannot explain but was universally expressed by our family was how much it meant to us that people attended the funeral. Some of our friends chose to not come because they did not know what to say or how to react to such a tragedy. What people need during this time is not some eloquent speech, mini-sermon, or Bible verses thrown at them. What people need in times of loss is to know you are sorry, you love them, and you are there just to sit and hold their hand or meet some obvious need. They just need to know you are there.

This is a list of the books that really helped me in the days following Micah's passing. The firsthand accounts of life on the other side were so meaningful to me that I would like to pass some of my favorites on to you.

- *Final Quest*, Rick Joyner
- *My Glimpse of Eternity*, Betty Maltz
- *Through Heaven's Gates*, Rebecca Springer
- *Return from Tomorrow*, George G. Ritchie
- *To Heaven and Back*, Rita Bennett

Also 2 newer books:

- *Glimpses of Heaven*, Trudy Harris, RN
- *Heaven is for Real*, Todd Burpo

I found that the mental portrait that really pulled us through was the reality of heaven. It is like the story of Peter when he saw Jesus walking out on the water. As long as he kept his eyes on Jesus, he was also able to walk on the water. But as soon as he looked at the wind and the waves, he began to sink. As long as we kept our minds on the fact that Micah was in heaven, we did not have to suffer with grief. The books that we read all strengthened our faith in and knowledge of heaven.

For My Good

BY DEBORAH GILES

What man meant for evil God meant for good...

Genesis 50:20

Trust was a key ingredient in our walking through this fiery furnace. Trust according to the dictionary means

> Assured reliance on the character, ability and strength or truth of someone or something. One in which confidence is placed. Dependence on something future; Hope. Something committed or entrusted to one to be used or cared for in the interest of another (Webster's Dictionary).

As we were tried in the fire, we were pleased to find out where our trust was.

I am very comforted by the scripture "All things work together for good for those who love the Lord and those who are called according to His purpose" (Romans 8:28). I know that all of us involved loved the Lord so losing a child is obviously for my good and for the good of others. Nothing is more comforting to me than scripture like this that speak directly to my heart. "All things" includes the death of my son.

Having gone through this trial, I am assured that I would not want my trust in anything else. In a time of trial, you also find out what you really believe. There is no way for me to overemphasize that I am what I eat. When the trial came, God's Word was what carried me through. Jesus joined with me in this test of all tests and became one with me.

I trust God with my life and that of my family. I am no longer afraid of death or what that separation can do to me. It has no hold on me. Eternity is real.

A Bible story that means a lot to me is the story of Joseph. Here is a man who was beloved of his father and envied by his brothers. His brothers decide to rid themselves of him once and for all. They try to kill him and then opt to sell him into slavery. Joseph goes through trials of injustice that I can hardly imagine. In the midst of everything, Joseph continues with life, always doing his best, always ending up on top. Then when he is reunited with those that tried to destroy him, all he sees is that what they had meant for evil, God had used for good. How many of us could be that pure? Some of these painful events that happened could have made him bitter, hateful, or angry. If he had drowned himself in self-pity I don't believe he would have been in a position to save his family when the famine came.

Joseph is really one of the great Bible role models. He obviously set his mind to serve and make the best out of life. I have a belief that cream always rises to the top. There is nothing you can do to stop it. Joseph was cream!

Detours and Dead Ends

BY DEBORAH GILES

*Yesterday is history.
Tomorrow is a
mystery. And
today? Today is a
gift; that's why they
call it the present.*

—Unknown

Life is an exciting journey. It has times of mountain climbing and times of sitting beside still waters. We are all on our own footpath with the Lord leading the way. Early in my Christian experience I saw this footpath. In my vision of this path, I could only see right in front of me. I remember watching Jesus's feet in front of me leading the way. I could not see ahead of Him on the path, I could only see him. He said He is the way. During this experience, I tried to stay close to Him on this path so He could show me the way. I believe that He did just that.

In the days and months since Micah's death, we have seen the devastation of not following Jesus as we walk through life's greatest trials. We have seen people who have taken detours that have taken them years down a road of their own choosing. One of these roads is the road of "*Why?*" God does not desire to hide truth from his children. We cannot demand to receive this information on our timetable, but His. If we insist on traveling down that road without Him we will be lost. He is the truth, so He desires to show you why. Sometimes we think we need to know something, and it is simply not

119

the right time. To learn something out of the timetable of God is not wise.

> There is an appointed time for
> everything. And there is a time for
> every event under heaven—
> A time to give birth and a time to die;
> A time to plant and a time to
> uproot what is planted.
> A time to kill and a time to heal;
> A time to tear down and a time to build up.
> A time to weep and a time to laugh;
> A time to mourn and a time to dance.
> A time to throw stones and a
> time to gather stones;
> A time to embrace and a time
> to shun embracing.
> A time to search and a time
> to give up as lost;
> A time to keep and a time to throw away.
> A time to tear apart and a
> time to sew together;
> A time to be silent and a time to speak.
> A time to love and a time to hate;
> A time for war and a time for peace.
>
> Ecclesiastes 3:1-8

We found timing is everything in God's economy.

Another detour is grief. He has promised to carry all our grief and sorrows. Also, He has told us He does not want us to grieve like those who have no hope. If we insist on carrying this load, He will allow it. In Ecclesiastes, it clearly states that there is a time for mourning to end. You will always miss your loved one, but you do not always have to be in the pain of grief and mourning.

Let your loved one go. I experienced the pain of letting Micah go the winter before he died. Micah came home one night after church and informed us that he was moving to Arizona to live with his friend Joey. He was leaving in two days. The turmoil that I experienced was agonizing. I begged him not to go. The night before he left, I stayed up almost all night. I prayed and wrote Micah a letter that he later referred to as my poison pen letter. This time was more painful to me than his death. The following is the letter I wrote him that night. He had saved the letter, and I found it in his room the morning we found his body.

The Poison Pen Letter

Dear Micah,

As a parent my greatest desire for my children is that they will grow up into a mature adult with a passion to follow after God and His purposes for their lives. Your father and I love you and want to help you avoid all the mistakes we have made and all the detours we have taken on the road to God's will. You have always pushed to take the hard road. Your desire to reject loving guidance has resulted in many painful miles for you and a broken and burdened heart for me.

We have no desire to live our lives through our children. Experience has taught me that when I am driven, it is the enemy of my soul at work. The Holy Spirit leads. He is not in a great hurry. Pushing and shoving me to make a quick and reckless decision.

This decision you have made to move away (a major life change) was made literally in a matter of hours with no input from those who love and cherish your soul.

I will never forget the time you and I talked after you were kicked out of school, and I was feverishly trying to get you into a home school program. You told me "why do you care? I don't care." I was looking down the road to the day that your classmates would be graduating and you would still have another year in school. You could not see that day but I could. Parents have long-range visibility.

At this moment, I can see the day when you will again wake up on someone else's couch and remember that you have a loving home with a bed and food and fellowship with a family who loves and cares for you more than you are seeing at this moment in your life. All you see are people telling you what to do. If you are not disciplined, the Bible says that you are a bastard. When a parent loves you, they discipline you. You are kicking against the discipline of your parents.

I truly believe that you have a call on your life, and like Jonah you are again running from God. You are in a cycle of making the same mistake over and over again. Life is a classroom, when you fail a test you do not move on to the next class…you have to keep taking the same test over and over until you get it right. Please do not do this thing you are about to do. Stay here, pass this test, and move on to the next classroom. You are weeks away from leaving home with your parents blessing. Honor your father and mother in this thing and you will reap the benefits. Drop your pride, humble yourself, and submit to your parents and the ministers who are watching over your soul.

Being a man is more than having your own house and paying your own bills. For you, it will be emptying yourself and becoming a servant.

Bible college will not make you a minister, but it will afford you the opportunity to dig into the word, learn the whole truth, and become skillful at rightly dividing God's word. When you got out of AUM (Auburn University Montgomery) you longed to get away to seek God with fasting and prayer. So far you have squandered that time, which led to my insisting on you getting a job.

The years are swiftly flowing through the hourglass. You can stay, honor your parents, complete your education, and launch into life with the blessings of God and your parents, or you can, as you put it, become your own man (self-made man), resist your parents, resist our God, and do it your way. There is no doubt you will make enough to provide shelter and food. But why settle for just that? Life is more than food and clothes.

What can we do to make this work? Like the woman said to us that night at Leigh's home, "it is as if it's over and it happens again." Please let it be over. Don't do this thing. God's call for you is mighty; don't run from it—run to it.

There is perfect peace and joy in God's perfect will. When Zavie and David married we had perfect peace and joy. Our little bird left the nest in God's perfect time, and in His will. I have no peace and no joy in your decision (neither do you if you will be honest with yourself). My little bird is flying into a storm.

Ponder my thoughts.

I love you,

Mom

The reason that this was so painful was I had to learn how to let him go. A day or so after Micah left for Arizona I was really suffering from grief. Christmas was near, and I did not even want to decorate or prepare for the holiday. One morning, as I was coming home from taking Stephen to school, I realized life does goes on. I saw so clearly that I had to let go of Micah and pay attention to the loved ones I still had. If I had followed my emotions we would have had a miserable holiday. I made the decision to go all out and provide a happy holiday for my family that was still with me.

What If—this could possibly be the most tormenting thought process that a person can get drawn into. Once you start traveling down this road it becomes self-propitiating. What if this, what if that, and if only this, if only that. People could save themselves endless miles of torment if they would get off this road at the next available exit. This only serves to undermine faith. God is sovereign. I had one friend ask me why God did not show us that this was about to happen so we could pray to stop it. My response is that if God had wanted us to prevent this, He would have. Saying "what if" is a dead end street because at the end of that road is emotional death. God is both sovereign and omnipotent or He is not. My strong conclusion is to resist the temptation of going down the dead end street named "what if."

Self Pity—there are times all of us have experienced self-pity about losing Micah. What we have tried to do is identify it when it comes. To indulge in self-pity turns us into bitter and ungrateful people. Self Pity is a dead end street as well or it can serve as a detour prolonging our much needed healing from the loss.

These are two streets (what if and self pity) you want to avoid; it is a recipe for emotional disaster awaiting you at the end of this dead end street.

Dealing with the Hard Questions

By DEBORAH GILES

Trials are medicines which our gracious and wise physician prescribes because we need them, and he proportions the frequency and weight of them to what the case requires. Let us trust his skill and thank him for his prescription.

—Isaac Newton

For me, the fact that I felt like Micah hastened his death troubled me for weeks. John had a very poignant dream during this time that said it all.

In the dream, John was walking down a new street. He had come to a dead end and he decided that he would cut through the woods at the end of the street. Just before he stepped off the sidewalk, he heard a voice say, "Hey, Dad." He looked over to the house at the end of the street and saw a group of people he did not know in the yard. Micah was with these people. He signaled for John to join them. John refused because he did not know the group Micah was with. Micah came to the end of the driveway to visit with John. John saw in the dream a low wall separating them from each other. Micah told John that he had just taken a test and had not done well on it. As he talked, he became a little whimpering boy. He said he had wagered bets on the test and was unable to pay up. He needed John's help.

The dream was really a picture of what had happened to Micah. It was as though Micah had been required to sit down and take an exam about his life choices. Micah had failed many of these test questions about his decisions, but this one exam question was fatal. Most youths feel that they are invincible. The test Micah failed cost him his life. Now it is up to us to pay off the wagers.

I have done a lot of soul searching to try to discover the fine line between grace and predestination. I wish I could tell you that I have discovered the secrets to life. What I have discovered is that we are saved by grace and not by any works that we can boast about. We all have human frailties. I have come to accept that God made Micah just the way he was. He even knew the weaknesses that Micah would struggle with.

As I look back on all the little things that I felt about Micah while he was here with me, I see that this was always the plan. Many times, I have had the thought that Zavie and Stephen would always live here near me, but I always felt Micah would grow up and leave. I thought that he would belong to the world because of ministry or calling. I know that there are several instances in the Bible where God changed His mind about His plan for someone's life. In the story of King Hezekiah, God sent the prophet Isaiah to him (2 Kings 20). Isaiah told him he would die and to set his affairs in order. The king pleaded for more time, and God granted his request. The king did not want to die as a result of his ignoring the prophet. I know that my son had a keen prophetic sense about the precepts of God. That being said, if God had showed Micah that he was going to take him home what would seem to most as an early departure like in the case of King Hezekiah, I doubt that Micah would have argued with him. As my loving Father, I can accept His all knowing decision.

SEVEN LESSONS WE LEARNED
At The Death of Our Nineteen-Year-Old Son

By JOHN W. GILES

The safest place to be is within the will of God.

—Unknown

After reading the chapters on 'Shucking Corn" and "Looking for Divine Signs and Fingerprints," we can draw so many real life experiences from these examples. Shortly after Micah's departure, I found myself wanting to put together a First Aid Kit, if you will, to those who I knew suffered a loss. It would be healing for me to reach out to those hurting with the breaking news of losing a loved one. This kit would always include a hand-written note from me, the booklet we had printed of the Collection of Writings by Micah, and this two-page write up on the "Seven Lessons We Learned." Recipients of the First Aid Kits always pointed out that the "Seven Lessons We Learned" was easy to read during those first few days of numbness. If one wanted to reduce this book down into a few bullet points, these seven lessons would probably be the best summary.

These seven lessons became an inspiration to my family. I trust these lessons will be of some comfort in knowing and experiencing the awesomeness of our God.

1 "Trust in the Lord with all of your heart, lean not unto your own understanding and in all your ways acknowledge Him and He will direct your paths" (Proverbs 3: 5&6). If we were ever going to trust God's decisions, we needed to trust him now. His decision to take Micah home would not have even been a multiple choice option for me, but God did not consult us before Micah's departure. We must trust our loved ones and friends to the sovereignty of God Almighty and not ever question His wisdom.

2 "All things work together for the good of those who love God and are called according to His purpose" (Romans 8:28). When I see what God has done through Micah's death, I stand in awe of *His* greatness and amazing way of taking something so horrific to the natural mind and causing so much good to come from it—even in the midst of so much pain and heartache. Many lives have been renewed in their faith, homes and marriages restored, and doors opened for the gospel from this life. John 12: 23-26 is true: "And Jesus said, 'Truly, truly I say unto you, unless a grain of wheat falls into the earth and dies, it remains by itself alone; but if it dies, it bears much fruit. He who loves his life loses it; and he who hates his life in this world shall keep it to life eternal. If anyone serves Me, let him follow Me; and where I am, there shall My servant be also be; if anyone serves Me, the Father will honor him.'"

3 "His Grace is sufficient for us and His strength is made perfect in our weaknesses" (2 Corinthians 12:9). This was a direct impact on me, much like the Titanic connecting with the iceberg, I was knocked down on the deck. We find in life people say I am going to lift you up in prayer. Lifting your need to the Lord is indeed one thing, but as the prayers go up somehow the burden is given levity as well. In our case, the Christian friends who were praying for us helped us carry this burden. In simple terms, our burden seemed dispersed over the shoulders of many versus our own shoulders.

4 "Be anxious for nothing, but by prayer and supplication with thanksgiving, let your request be known unto God and the peace of God that passes all understanding will keep your hearts and minds through Jesus Christ" (Philippians 4: 6-7). If we ever needed peace, now was our appointed time. God's supernatural peace permeated our home, the visitation at the funeral home, our entire family, friends, the church, and the gravesite. God's unquestionable peace stilled the troubled waters of our souls.

5 "Never say 'What if'." When we were on our way to the wreck site after the Alabama State Trooper helicopter found Micah's Jeep, my wife and I were riding together. I was very quiet thinking about all of my next twenty steps and what was going to be required of me, and she softly said, "John, we

have been married for twenty-seven years, and for twenty-four of those, we have been faithfully walking with Him. He will see us through all of this." There was a pause and she said this, "Let's make each other a promise right now before we get to the wreck and as we walk through all of this, let's never say 'what if'." These two words were inspiration to us, for these small words have been the most powerful of all in our walk through this endeavor. These two words have kept us from questioning the sovereignty of God, His wisdom, His direction and have protected us from falling into deep grief and self-pity. Never say "what if?"

6 "Have no unfinished business. Owe no man anything but to love him" (Romans 13:8). As I sat on our sofa about twenty-five minutes after leaving the wreck site, friends were pouring in the house, and I was pondering over the fast moving events of the afternoon. The thought occurred to me as I sat on that sofa with my family, and I blurted out to those with us there, "You know what is so good about all of this—we had no unfinished business." I realized that Micah owed no man anything but to love them, he had no unfinished business. Around our house, and I hope it is like this around your house, we say I love you to each other about 250 times a day. Even our parrot will say "Love y'all" when we go out the door in the morning. Even when Micah hung up the phone from

his friends he would say, "I love you." Please do not let the sun go down on your anger; it will only defile you and those around you. Owe no man anything but to love them.

7 "Keep him alive" We found it healthy to talk about Micah all the time as a family. Some choose to not talk about the lost loved ones, but we felt keeping him alive in our thoughts was healthy. It is bad enough losing a child, but to not talk about them was worse from our perspective. It would almost seem like he never existed. We would laugh and laugh about his personality traits and habits we all found comical. Our friends were very patient with us when we would go out to dinner and all we talked about was Micah. Keeping Micah alive was good for us.

We trust this book has in some way blessed you. There is hope because Jesus has promised His return. We will meet Micah again one day, and you will see your loved ones again. Trust the Lord and give Him your heart and life.

Conclusion

By JOHN AND DEBORAH GILES

*God had one son
on earth without
sin, but never one
without suffering.*

—Saint Augustine

*True, I am in love
with suffering, but
I do not know if I
deserve the honor.*

—Saint Ignatius

*We always find that
those who walked
closest to Christ were
those who had to bear
the greatest trials.*

—Saint Teresa
of Avila

*Suffering is the very
best gift He has to give
us. He gives it only to
His chosen friends.*

—Saint Therese
of Lisieux

In conclusion, all parents have the thought cross their mind at some point of how they would deal with losing a child. These thoughts are fleeting as they flash across our minds. We would like for any thoughts like these to dissipate immediately out of our mind.

Micah was a passionate young man who had a heart like King David in the Old Testament, who sought after the heart of God. He also had a dark side like King David. Micah did have clay feet and was not perfect to say the least. While he had positive attributes to impact the world for Christ, he also had negative attributes as he would go out of his way and disobey God and sometimes swim to the dark island. There are good and bad lessons he taught us all.

It is our hope that you can find this book useful in dealing with the losses in life. Somehow, some way we were spared from the deep hollows of grief. Learning to never say "what if" was huge. Discovering the path to view death as the gateway to eternity is a critical component. Keeping an eternal perspective about death versus a temporal, earthly view is paramount in the battle over grief.

It has been over ten years since we said goodbye to Micah. When he first left us we did not think a day could go by without him being ever in our thoughts. We have to admit that whole days go by without our minds wondering toward Micah. Life does go on, and the pain ends and is replaced by the happy memories.

He is never closer than when we are at church praying. The reality of the communion of saints has become very precious and real to us. Each year as we grow older we say goodbye to those we love as they cross that river and join the cloud of witnesses. As we gather around the altar and tabernacle at church, we are reminded of all our loved ones who are present with Christ face to face. When we are gathered together at church in prayer, we sense their presence. We know that they are interceding for us and cheering us on in this life.

Our prayer is that anyone who hears our testimony will be filled with the hope that heaven is real and that our loved ones live on. We each face the loss of loved ones differently as you can see even from the different ways that we behaved in loosing Micah. Some of the things that we did to get closure would have tormented some. We each must follow that still small voice of the Lord and do whatever he tells us. There is no magic formula; our testimony is only a template of ideas that worked for us. Maybe something that we learned can be of assistance in helping you find that peace in your own heart.

We also discovered that suffering has a vital role in forming us into the image of Christ. For the first twenty-plus years of our Christian walk, we had never heard this taught. Suffering purges our sins. It makes us look closely into the mirror of our soul and see who we really are. Hebrews 5:8 tells us that suffering teaches us obedience. It can bring us to an understanding of how we have caused suffering in the lives of others and bring us to repentance.

If we do not understand the importance suffering plays in our life, we will avoid it at all cost, which could cause us to turn to artificial means of escape. Being armed with the knowledge that suffering is chiseling the rough edges out of our life we can lean into the pain and let it have its perfect result. Suffering is not continuous for most of us. It comes and goes in life, giving us times of rest between trials.

Suffering also brings us into closer unity with Christ. As we walk out our own sufferings, we understand more intensely what he suffered for us. We understand more about the price He paid for us. Our prayers previous to loosing Micah were prayers of request. We had never been taught about entering into Christ, suffering in prayer. As we began practicing this form of meditations on the crucifixion, we found it to be life changing. These past years have been a class room of entering into his suffering both in prayer and meditation on the events of Christ's final days on this earth. He invited us to come with Him and take up our cross and follow Him. It isn't a popular message or an invitation that sounds fun, but it is the invitation. It is the way to become His disciple. A life patterned after His life of selfless sacrifice for the love of others.

Finally, entering into suffering is redemptive. Isn't that why he brought us into His family, so that we can help Him bring redemption to this fallen and hurting world? As we suffer with Him for others, we cease our selfish pursuits and place our eyes on helping those that Christ has placed in our life to help. God's ways are not like our ways. It is through the door of suffering that you enter into glory. In this life, we spend much of our time avoiding this path at all cost. Yet this is the real path to the riches of His glory. So take heart, all of your suffering will bring you closer to Christ and His glory. All of your suffering will someday be replaced with a crown.

Micah Worthington Giles, Senior Picture, Lanier
High School 1998

Little Micah—about 3 years old—trying to get his composure for the photo

Micah and Grandmother Giles after a Patsy
Cline Reenactment, Alabama Shakespeare
Festival, Montgomery, Alabama

Giles Family Photo—November 1993—Front Row: Deborah, John, Zaviera. Back Row: Stephen, Micah.

Micah Kills 8 Point Buck—Sumter County Alabama 1999—Left to Right: Pastor Lamar Golden, Micah, Stephen, and John. The Jeep Micah was killed in is behind us.

Micah & Granddaddy Giles before a piano concert that Micah was performing in. Micah was about 9 years old here

Micah in a bell choir at Trinity Presbyterian Church. Mary Margaret Petranka was fourth to the right. We did not even know he volunteered for this choir. He was about 16 years old in this picture.

Zaviera (Zavie), Micah, and Stephen, living room of our home, 4 doors from the Governor's Mansion. Micah was about 17 years old here in this photo.

Micah and John after Patsy Cline Reenactment, Alabama Shakespeare Festival Montgomery, Alabama. Grandmother Giles studio apartment at Eastdale Retirement Home

Deborah, Micah, and Zavie. Micah just won first place, Guide On Competition, Lyman Ward Military Academy

Micah, Life Chain Montgomery, Micah was about 12 years old

Micah, 17 and Stephen, 14

Due to the mud on the back of the jeep and the east sun shadow cast on this side of the interstate, the Jeep was camouflaged from the morning helicopter fly over. In this photo, Micah was still in the Jeep, laying over the console into the front passenger seat before the authorities opened the sealed cabin after three days in the heat.

The impact into the concrete and steel pylon brought the Jeep to an immediate halt. The collision drove the steering wheel into the front seat, catapulting Micah into the passenger door and instantaneously breaking his neck.

Montgomery Advertiser

Obituaries

Alabama Heritage Funeral Home
Robert Moulton, III 215-0180

Giles, Micah Worthington, born on June 12, 1979, departed this life May 15, 1999. He is survived by his father and mother, John and Deborah Giles, a sister and brother-in-law, Zaviera and David George, and a brother Stephen Chadwick Giles. He was preceded by his grandfathers, W.O. Giles, Sr., and John C. Woodley. He is also survived by his grandmothers, Mary E. Giles and Ruth Woodley, as a well as a great grandmother, Gurthrie Rowell. His other survivors are aunts and uncles: Caroline and Del Mixon,  Flowery Branch, GA, Bill and Margine Giles, Ted and Donna Giles of Montgomery, AL, Chess Woodley of Beaufort, SC, Jennifer and Tim Kannapel of Huntsville, AL. His cousins are Tre and Monica Giles and Allison and John LeFeve of Holly Pond, AL, Heather Perry of Augusta, GA and Wynn Giles of Montgomery, AL, James Noland and Elizabeth Noland of Auburn, AL and Amanda and Madison Kannapel of Huntsville, AL, Dustin Woodley, Autumn Woodley, Audrey Woodley, Anna Woodley, Anthony Woodley, Jessica Yates and Regina Yates, all of Beaufort, SC. He has numerous great aunts, uncles and second cousins. His best friend, Mary Margaret Petranka of Montgomery, AL also survives him. Micah was a very special young man and was loved by all that came to know him. From the beginning of his short life, we all knew he was special to the Lord. Micah attended Lyman Ward Military Academy, New Life Academy and Graduated in 1988 from Lanier High School. He attended Auburn University of Montgomery and Troy University in Montgomery. He previously owned and operated Grass Hopper Lawn Care Service. He was employed by G.T. Key Electrical Company. The family will receive friends at Alabama Heritage Funeral Home from 6:00 p.m. until 8:00 p.m. in the evening on Wednesday, May 19, 1999. Services will be officiated by Father Jim Pinto of Birmingham, AL, at Frazer Memorial United Church at 1:00 p.m. on Thursday, May 20 with interment at Alabama Heritage Cemetery. Memorials may be made to Sav-A-Life of Montgomery or Christian Coalition of Alabama.

Alabama Heritage Directing

Part 2

Memorials
and Landmarks

If you read history you will find that the Christians who did the most for the present world were precisely those who thought most of the next. It is since Christians have largely ceased to think of the other world that they have become so ineffective in this.

—C.S. Lewis

From Deborah

I have never given much thought to cemeteries or grave markers. When my father died I was the family member in residence here in Montgomery, so the responsibility fell on me to make the arrangements.

He left no instructions, so a simple stone with his name and dates and with information about his military service seemed appropriate. After Micah died, looking at most headstones, they just seemed so sterile for a life that had so much to say. The family was in much discussion about the matter. The children and I wanted a headstone with his name and his restaurant message. John wanted Micah's full name on the headstone. After numerous conversations the children and I won out. A couple of nights later Stephen had a dream where Micah told him that he liked what we had decided to do for his marker. That settled it.

This past year when my sister was in town visiting, we were trying to think of an interesting activity for her children. My niece, Amanda, is a real history buff so I suggested a visit to our oldest cemetery, where civil war soldiers are buried. We strolled through the civil war graves and then made our way up to the old family plots. It seemed as though every life had a story. Not just names and dates, but meaningful quotes and scriptures. Every life was a message left for future generations to read. You saw the tragedy of a lost family member and the faith of those left behind.

One plot was especially beautiful, and we wandered through it for probably thirty minutes. We were very surprised to discover that someone had been buried there that year. An iron fence surrounds it; the gate has the family name in it. There is jasmine planted all around the fence with dogwood trees planted on two corners. When you enter the plot, there is a beautiful stone and iron cross in the center. The ground is paved with various sizes and shapes of marble and granite stones. This is where the beauty comes in; each stepping-stone has a message. It is either a meaningful quote or a scripture or the words of a hymn. Every word carved in stone for generations yet unborn to read—a testimony of faith for all to see. I was inspired just reading what these people had left behind for me to know about them.

Right before we wrapped up our field trip to the cemetery, my sister spotted someone entering the plot. We took off across the cemetery to meet the visitor. The plot was hers; her husband had designed and built it as a Christmas gift to her many years earlier. Her husband had died that previous fall and was now buried there. She shared with us how sometimes she and her husband would wake up in the morning, make coffee, and go up there. You could tell that years of thought and effort had gone into this gift of love—a gift not only to her but also to future generations.

I know that cost prohibits us from returning to the time of costly family plots. There is a lesson to be learned from those who have gone on before us. They spent more time than we do considering the hereafter and planning a final resting place. Something to consider is the fact that once you die, your home at some point will be passed on and all your belongings lost to a yard sale somewhere. The only place where you can continue to speak will probably be your grave marker.

Several summers ago I attended a ladies luncheon at a conference in California. When I arrived and saw the program, I couldn't believe how many people were going to speak. They were charismatic Episcopal Bishops' wives, and each was asked to share their favorite scripture and tell why it was their favorite. It was probably one of the best meetings I have ever attended. Each testimony was more inspiring than the last. It made me question what one or two sentences would I like to leave behind that would let others know who I am?

From John

Deborah, Stephen, and I (and our niece, Amanda Kannapel) went to Israel in 1999 after Micah's death to reflect and make a pilgrimage to our Christian roots— something we had always wanted to do. There were a few things I needed to complete relative to Micah's death when I returned from Israel. First, we strongly felt the need to have a head stone dedication service consecrating this earthly stone for ministry. Many people over the years would view Micah's headstone as they visited the graves of loved ones, and we wanted his message on this earthen rock dedicated for God's service. It was obvious we needed to hold a special service. It seemed a bit different, but many felt this was an inspired idea and very appropriate.

The other expression that I felt compelled to complete upon returning from Israel was placing a cross with Micah's name at the location of the wreck. This story follows the Head Stone Consecration explanation.

At the time, we thought we were holding a dedication service consecrating this stone to speak to people as they visited the cemetery. We wanted to dedicate this rock that had been carved with human hands and have the message on the stone blessed to continue forever Micah's work. Little did we realize we were tapping deep into the traditions of the Jewish culture by unveiling this stone.

All who profess the Christian faith fully recognize and acknowledge that our heritage is born right out of the roots of Jewish customs. The Jewish tradition is steeped in a deep sense of understanding and meaning when dealing with death and mourning. In another segment of this book we discuss the Jewish customs of handling grief, but here I wanted to touch on the unveiling of the tombstone.

It is customary for the grave marker to be put in place and for an unveiling ceremony to be held by the end of one year after the burial of a loved one. The unveiling ceremony consists of the recitation of Psalms, a very brief eulogy capsulating the most salient characteristics of the deceased and then removing the cloth covering the headstone. Also it was a custom to leave a small stone or rock rather than flowers. Rocks are a marker of remembrance and they do not fade or wither. In addition it is a sign that someone has visited. It was also common to write a note and tuck the paper into a crevice of the stone somewhere.

If there was no crevice, the note would be weighted down with a stone.

All of that being said, when we were in Israel we did see small rocks on the Jewish tombs. We noticed that people would leave rocks and notes at Micah's grave. It meant a great deal to our family to see these rocks and notes.

When we had the consecration service for the stone, it seemed a little odd even to us to have this done. Now that we know about the Jewish customs, we feel it was an inspired idea.

Robbie Morton with Heritage Funeral Home was so gracious to set up a tent and chairs for this service. It was an anointed time to set this rock apart for its work for the kingdom. Below is a copy of the program that we passed out at the service that explains why we had the stone made in such a specific and meaningful manner for our family.

Micah Worthington Giles

Head Stone Consecration—
Dedication Service
May 20, 2000
2:00 p.m.
Heritage Funeral Home & Cemetery
10505 Atlanta Hwy.
Montgomery, AL (334) 215-0180

Head Stone Consecration—
Dedication Service

PURPOSE

The purpose of this ceremony is to set aside this earthly stone for divine service unto the Lord and to continue the ministry of one of His young servants, Micah Worthington Giles. This stone encapsulates a story of a young, prophetic evangelist, his message, and his ministry

MAY 15, 1999

May 15, 1999 marks the day of Micah's automobile accident and being transformed from this life into life eternal. It also marks the anniversary date of the Israeli's Independence Day, which was also Micah's Independence Day. May is our fifth month and the Israeli third month. Five in scripture means grace, and we will be discussing three in a moment.

HEAD STONE CONSTRUCTION

The Head Stone was built five feet and ten and a half inches high. Micah's driver's license stated that he was five feet nine, but the forensic science report indicated he was five feet and eleven and a half inches tall. We built the monument five feet and ten and a half inches to replicate Micah's height. The stone was cut and not finished in the normal high gloss finish and the edges were cut with rough edges as well. The purpose in this was to communicate that Micah was a fine stone still in the rough. He was tough, fearless, loved the outdoors, camping, fishing and was a skilled hunter. The stone was broken on an angle to illustrate that Micah did not live a full term life. We had the stone shaped like a rock because he was hard as a rock, built his spiritual life on the rock, Jesus Christ, and he loved to jump off of Chimney Rock on Lake Martin.

THREE LAYER STONE

We purposely constructed the head stone in three pieces. As we look back on Micah's life, we see many examples of where the number three played a major role as he worked diligently to walk like the Lord Jesus. Micah had been walking with the Lord in his new ministry for three years, he had been back from Arizona for three months, we used to joke about him being Jonah, he was missing for three days, he was called home by the Lord on the third calendar month according to Hebrew custom, we put three transmissions in his truck which was a family joke, and the list goes on. Jesus too was in ministry only three years, and he arose after the third day. So in our family, when it comes to Micah and the number three, it is significant.

Ten Inches Thick

The Head Stone is ten inches thick. Ten in scriptures means responsibility on earth or completeness. We all trusted in the sovereignty of God taking Micah home because his responsibility and work on earth was completed.

Scripture on the Front

Father Jim Pinto consecrating Micah's headstone, Heritage Cemetery

Many recall that Micah would stand up in restaurants, whistle to get everyone's attention, and then give them a forty-second message. The inscription on the front of the stone is intended to preach to all who pass by. On the secondary base stone, we see the inscription, "Who is like the Lord?" This is the biblical meaning of the name Micah. Micah lived everyday of his last three years of his life trying to live up to his name—to be "like the Lord."

Scripture on the Back

This scripture is taken directly from Micah 6:8. It is our challenge from the Old Testament Prophet Micah to do justice, to love mercy, and to walk humbly before our God.

Trumpet Player

As we find in scripture and in the historical church, the trumpets were a call to worship at the temple and also a call to war either with the trumpet or the shofar horn. Micah as an evangelist did sound the trumpet. Also, Micah was a worshipper, for the last thing he would do when he went to bed was to play three or four worship songs. And when he woke up, on his way out the door to work or school, he would play again. For those who believe in modern day prophecy, Micah received a word one evening that his ministry would be like a trumpet. We felt that the trumpet was a symbol that played a significant role in Micah's life, so we included this sketch on the stone.

Footstone

The footstone carries Micah's full name, the dates spanning his life on earth, and a picture of this handsome young man. Maybe we are biased and not very objective, but we believe he was and is a very handsome young man.

The Cross I-65 South

Prior to going to Israel, I had made this huge cross to put at the interstate wreck site. Deborah and Zavie gave me a hard time because the cross was large enough for Jesus to be crucified on. I mean to tell you it was huge. I knew without question that I was to get that cross erected as soon as we got home from Israel. It was just something I had to do.

We got home, and the next Sunday morning at four-thirty, I was up and on my way to put up this huge cross that normally would take two Roman soldiers to carry. I hurriedly took the posthole diggers, installed the cross, and hit the road. I felt such satisfaction and completion.

Monday morning, Deborah took Stephen to School in Millbrook, and on her way back she noticed the cross was missing. I went to check it out, and you would not believe what had happened. In less than 24 hours after I installed the cross, it was apparent another wreck had taken place in the same place. The cross had been clipped by the vehicle and had tumbled down the embankment and laid propped up against the bridge pillar. This was so strange and it was obvious the car had rolled down the hill by all of the evidential broken glass and debris.

I trimmed down the size of the cross and returned it to the site and reinstalled it once again. A few weeks later, another wreck took place at the same site and the cross was down again. Danny Day, a plumber from Elmore County who was part of our search and rescue posse hunt for Micah, called me one day and said the cross was down. He asked me if he could repair the cross and put it in a heavy cast iron pipe that he would submerge in the ground. I was so grateful for his help, and to this day, it still stands beside bridge number five on I-65 South.

Funeral Eulogy

By RICK BLACKERBY

*I would rather
have a plain coffin
without a flower,*

*A funeral
without a eulogy,
than a life without
the sweetness of
love and sympathy.*

*Let us learn to
anoint our friends
beforehand for
their burial.*

*Post-mortem
kindness does
not cheer the
burdened spirit.*

*Flowers on
the coffin cast
no fragrance
backward over
the weary way.*

—George
William Childs

Rick Blackerby's eulogy began with reading the lyrics from Garth Brooks' Song "Fit For A King."

FIT FOR A KING

His pulpit's
the corner of
Nineteenth
and Main

His grip on the
gospel is his one
claim to fame.

As he offers
salvation through
the Savior on high.

"Fit or a King" is a song about a street preacher who is not a pretty picture, needs a bath, looks a little wild, and is fighting the in climate weather as he preaches his heart out on the street corner. He talks about one day at the end of time, the angels will be singing as if to say, "well done" and the rag clothes he was wearing on earth would one day be fit for a king.

Rick Blackbery read this song with passion because he started out street preaching and he identified with Micah. Here is his account of the story of meeting Micah in his own words:

> I'm an evangelist. I met Micah Giles just across the way preaching at a college revival for Frazer Memorial. He came up to reacquaint himself because our parents knew one another, and he was rejoicing because of his recent commitment to live wholeheartedly for Jesus. He was so excited. He said, "Rick, I've been preaching publicly." And I thought, "Wow!" I started at about his age sharing the gospel on the streets of Atlanta, and I said, "Another young man with boldness and zeal for the gospel of Jesus." He said, "No, that's not what I mean, Rick." He said, "I've been standing up in restaurants, like Outback, and I just whistle, and I get everyone's attention, and I share a brief message about Jesus."
>
> I said to myself in the back of my mind, "That's odd," and I wasn't comfortable. All my life is spent preaching Jesus. I live to see people come to the Lord, but I wasn't comfortable. I thought, *This guy's a little weird. Where's he going with this thing? He's a fanatic. What's he doing?* but I couldn't shake it. I went home, and I still couldn't shake it. There was something about the passion of his spirit—something about the purity of his

devotion—something about the clarity of his focus in life, so I called him. I said, "Micah, you're coming with me to Fort Walton. I've got to preach to some students after a football game, and if God would lead you, I want you to do what you've been doing, and I want to be there."

All the way down there I'd ask him questions. We were at Montgomery Mall, and I said, "When do you do it?"

"When Jesus tells me."

"Well what do you say?"

"What Jesus tells me to say."

I'm trying to find a hole in this somewhere. "Micah, why do you do this?"

"Because people are going to hell for eternity if I do not. And I love them Rick; I've gotta tell them."

We got to a little pizza place in Fort Walton, and the two ladies who met us, the coach's wife and a friend, took us out to dinner before the game. They took the "get-away car" option. He'd give people the option just to leave if they didn't want to participate. I wanted to participate. He stood in the middle of this small restaurant, and he whistled. Cokes and beer bottles and pizzas hit the table. I stood by the door shaking. I was embarrassed—I'm an evangelist.

He said, "Wide is the way to destruction, but narrow is the way to eternal life. And if you would bow your knee today and give your heart to Jesus as Lord of lords and King of kings, you too can be saved. Thank you, enjoy your dinner."

Micah lived more in twenty years than most of us will live in eighty to a hundred. If he were here, he would not celebrate his own perfection or some kind of moral accomplishment in life. He would encourage you to live with purity of devotion and ask you only to do what Jesus has told you to do.

Micah obeyed the greatest commandment: "Love the Lord your God with all your heart and strength and might and love your neighbor as yourself." Micah loved people, and that made him the winner in life.

Love Notes from Micah's Friends

After hundreds of notes and letters poured into our home expressing love to our family, we chose to take excerpts from some of these letters and notes so you might hear what others said about our Micah.

Streeter Wiatt
FAMILY FRIEND

"To obey is better than sacrifice" (1 Samuel 15:22). Micah was a living testimony to this scripture. You would not find Micah making righteous-looking sacrifices or doing religious looking acts. When God would tell Micah to "go" or "speak" he would obey. His conversion was true and deep and real and he cared not to impress God or man. He had a deep relationship with the God who saved him and he had the boldness of his namesake to proclaim the Lord he loved. I remember Micah, as a young believer, coming by my house one night. I invited him in and asked him what was on his mind. He broke down weeping and said that he wanted his friends to know the Jesus he knew. He said they needed Jesus, and he needed prayer to tell them about Jesus. There was a small group of believers at my house who gladly prayed for Micah and encouraged him and sent him off to testify of the one who had changed him.

Mr. Fiorini
MICAH'S TEACHER

I reflect back on Micah's life, and I remember him coming into the classroom with Jeremiah singing "Captain D's please!" I tried to keep them focused on geometry, but they would harmonize throughout the period. At least it wasn't a boring class. I was always amazed at Micah's reasoning and logic skills. Given a project, he could somehow manage to determine the outcome and it usually wasn't the way I had in mind, but his process was truly brilliant. After he left New Life, he came and told me how he was using what he learned in my geometry class to help his new teacher—I was so pleased to know he had learned. I also remember him standing on a chair in the lunchroom and speaking on the ills of drugs and proclaiming God's solution to the problem—Jesus. I miss Micah.

Alice Lewellan
FRIEND OF FAMILY

One of the sweetest pictures etched in my mind and on my heart is of your family taking communion at River of Life. Micah is there, of course, humble and intent, receiving of the life that is in the blood. What a picture you all make! Of all the families I witnessed, yours remains a strong memory, one that now testifies to me of the faith and security in Micah's heritage. Thank you for that testimony. It stands as a reminder of the depth and quality of love we have received and are called to pass on to our children. I am profoundly grateful for your example.

Darlene Bunch
MICAH'S AUNT

Micah is a beautiful soul; he had the ability to make you feel you were hugged without even touching you. He radiated love, and I was so glad to have met him, even though it was brief. A little of Micah goes a long way. He gave so much. God is with you.

Dr. Foch Smart
FAMILY FRIEND & ORTHODONTIST

I'm especially grateful because I feel like I got to know Micah and you and Stephen much better than I ever would have had I not seen you once a month. Micah was always such a joy when he came into the office. He seemed to feel "at home" and would clown around with us and with Stephen. It also gave me a real insight into the deep love that he and Stephen shared for each other. More than once, I heard Stephen say, "Hey, Micah, what color o-rings do I want today?" It was very obvious that Stephen loved and looked up to Micah, and that Micah loved him right back…One of the great goals of my life is to instill that kind of relationship between my kids.

Nicholas Adams
FAMILY FRIEND

Micah achieved much by the time of his death, and the work he did continues still in the hearts and in the deeds of those he touched. Micah lived up to his name. Much like the prophet Micah warned of God's destruction on the lands of Judah and Samaria unless they otherwise turned to God and away from their idolatry and sinful nature, Micah Giles realized that he too must tell others that they must turn to God if they seek eternal life and happiness. I believe Micah knew what the prophet Micah knew.

Christen Stephens
MICAH'S FRIEND

Micah brought a lot of joy into my life...Micah was a testimony to many people and reached out to help when people needed it the most, I know this because he helped me.

Glenda Householder
MICAH'S TEACHER

I remember the first time I saw Micah...He had such a big, warm smile as he took my hand and said, "Nice to meet you." As the year passed, I saw in Micah his love for life and mankind. I also realized he walked his life to a different beat, but one thing was certain, he knew the master drummer and that was Jesus! Micah was bold and bright and shared his feelings. He was very independent of man and very dependent on Jesus...this I admired greatly...I loved hearing Micah and Stephen share their hunting stories...they were quite a team.

Robert & Betsy Parker
FAMILY FRIEND

We witnessed some of the purposes God had for Micah. We watched Micah grow into such a fine young man whose influence on many of us will be a lasting testament to his life and his love for God and his family.

Derrell Vaughn
MICAH'S FRIEND

Micah was a great, young, mature man...A few years ago, after members of Trinity church had returned from a short term missions trip to Jamaica, I was asked to coordinate a Sunday evening service for those missionaries. I can't remember whether or not Micah went on that trip, but I do recall asking him to join David Bedsole in providing the music for the hour. Those boys were so willing, so humble, and so doggoned talented! After the service, an elder told me that it was the best Missions Report he had ever seen in all his years at Trinity. Micah played a part in leading him to that conclusion.

Penny Vickers
FRIEND OF THE FAMILY

The zeal of life was a great part of Micah and I will miss him. I sought the Lord about Micah, and He reminded me that Micah lived life to the fullest, pushing the limits of restrain.

Lori Smart
FAMILY FRIEND, WIFE OF ORTHODONTIST

Sometimes it takes quite a while for us to see the good from the bad that Romans 8:28 speaks of, but I want you to know that good is already occurring; I for one rededicated my walk. My sweetest memory of him was at a Wednesday night River of Life prayer meeting when he got up, led by the spirit, and picked out by ear a praise song on the piano and softly began singing. I remember once when we were without a pastor that someone had said that the least expected may prophesy; a few weeks later Micah shared a word, and I knew that "least expected" word was fulfilled in Micah.

John & Sue Tranter
FRIENDS OF FAMILY

Very soon after the news of Micah, a member of our prayer group emailed a request that we agree together that Micah be raised from the dead and returned to your family. As I joined in prayer, a brief glimpse of heaven caused me to write the prayer group and say I think Jesus will have a hard time convincing Micah to come back. I saw two young men, about the same age, sitting on the ground and engaging in a very intense and delightful discussion. They were completely healthy, happy, and obviously talking about something of special interest to them both. They seemed to be drawing on the ground. One was Micah, the other a young King David. The discussion was on the strategy of David's exploits over wild beasts and giants. They were not as teacher and student, but rather peers. The discussion involved give and take. Micah's contributions were well received and appreciated by David. They had a friendship like David had with Jonathan on this earth. This picture of Micah, totally fulfilled, wonderfully happy, and excited in heavenly participation, led me to thank God for His goodness and everlasting mercy.

Stephen's Song

"A Tribute to My Brother"
Written By Stephen C. Giles
Inspired by God and
Sung at Micah's Funeral

Micah I loved you so much.
Look around; see all the lives that you've
Touched.
From the twenty years you spent upon
the earth,
We knew it wasn't just an ordinary birth;
It was you, Micah Giles.
Mary Margaret, you've gotta hold on,
And we will see him before too long.
It will be a bittersweet sixteen,
But I know that he's living with the King.
I'm just glad that I got those fifteen years.
All the fun and sharing.
All the tears of our love,
Micah Giles

A Collection of Writings

By MICAH WORTHINGTON GILES

No two Christians will ever meet for the last time.

—Unknown

While John and his sister Caroline were in his office preparing for Micah's funeral, they came across these papers Micah had written for various school assignments both for high school and college. Copies of these writings were reproduced and available at the funeral for guests. After hearing about Micah in this book, we thought you might like to hear from him. These writings are placed by the date in which Micah had written them.

Schools and the Problems Therein

BY MICAH W. GILES
December 2, 1997

"Rare indeed is the child who has parents with love so wise and understanding, so objective, as to happily balance needed limits with the freedom to grow and develop the child's own talents, to allow realization of its full potential." (Shirley MacLaine). Schools are to be run in the same way a parent rears his child, which is something our society has lost. Three of the most prominent problems in the schools today are misbehavior in the classroom, teachers' lack of ability to discipline accordingly, and lack of communication between students and teachers.

Misbehavior usually stems from lack of proper guidance. Guidance starts in the home through a strong family who maintains strong values. Unfortunately guidance is not always present in the homes, which results in misbehavior in the classroom. This misbehavior in the classroom disrupts the learning process and needs to be dealt with through some form of disciplinary action.

Unfortunately teachers are not allowed the freedom in most cases to discipline as needed—especially in public school systems. Discipline, as defined by *Webster's Collegiate Dictionary*, is "*training* that corrects, molds, or perfects the mental faculties or moral character." Discipline at its peak performance is dispensed when the punishment fits the offense. In our system of law, a misdemeanor crime could not be corrected by capital punishment, and a felon could not be corrected by giving him a fifty-dollar fine. The same is true in our educational system. Talking out of order in class does not constitute suspension, and the use of drugs by a student should not be punished by a vacuum date. The use of improper discipline could result in a student being warp-minded of the reason for discipline. This could cause a child to grow up and become an abusive parent or a push-over to their children. It is our God-given duty to see that children learn what the true purpose of discipline is and how it benefits them.

The third problem found in schools is a lack of communication between students and teachers. If communication skills are not taught at schools, these students will have problems communicating for the rest of their lives. The result of this will be broken homes and scarred relationships with people in the work place. If a student feels that he cannot express the way he feels to a teacher, he will keep it "bottled up" on the inside. This causes students to feel that they are on one team, and the teachers are on another team in competition with one another. The teacher should make strides in this area to keep communication lines open. A teacher should never point out student's weaknesses in front of other students because it would make the student feel too insecure to tell a teacher how he is really feeling. At the same time, students should not undermine a teacher's authority over his classroom because this puts the teacher on the defensive.

Until the family unit can be welded back together, it is necessary for those in charge such as teachers to provide the appropriate discipline, guidance, and communication that a parent would provide to their child. As a leader a teacher should be an example to the student. There must be limits in the classroom, but at the same time, there must be the needed freedom for students to make decisions on their own and either suffer the consequences or reap the benefits for those decisions without hearing scorn or ridicule from the teacher.

Changed Forever

By MICAH W. GILES
October 4, 1998
English 101

The event that most dramatically changed my life is a very personal matter, but one that I am happy to share with you. Hopefully, this story will have the same impact on you that it had on me.

My parents always said that I was the perfect child up until around the age of eight. At that point, they said I began getting bitter towards authority. I lived a relatively sheltered life all through my childhood with basically no exposure to "the real world." Once in middle school, my mind began exploring the possibilities of a world beyond my little "eggshell." In the ninth grade, I was expelled from Faith Christian School for marking on the church pew with an ink pen. However, I had really given that school a hard time, and this episode was just the straw that broke the camel's back. I moved to New Life Christian School where I was suspended for having an empty bottle of wine on campus. By now, you can see what kind of trail I was walking down. My ninth grade summer was even worse. I turned fifteen and began stealing my sister's car after everyone was asleep. I would stay out until three-thirty in the morning either drinking, smoking pot, or both. However, my parents caught me several times and decided to send me to military school. Military school was an unpleasant experience. After about five good fights, most of which I lost, I decided I would rather be at home. Finally the year ended, and I came home for the summer. When I returned, I decided to change a few things. Instead of being so careless about my various "activities," I would be a little subtler. After all, I was sixteen years old and now had a car; it would now be much easier to sneak around, right? Wrong! Instead, I got caught with pot about three times. I was already back at New Life Academy so military school was not an option, at least not until the semester was over. Then one day, I flashed a bag of pot to the "wrong person" who told on me. My mom and dad stayed up until ten o'clock trying to get a confession out of me, and received it not. I had been sitting on the couch cushion that had all my goods under it. Knowing my dad was going to strip search me, I figured it would be a good idea. It worked and everybody went to bed. I got my pot and went upstairs to smoke it out of my window. My sister came in my room, saw what I was doing, and started screaming. I was kicked out of my house that night, and my wallet was taken from me. After three days away from home, I returned for my wallet. My parents stalled me and took me out to dinner. For whatever reason, I returned to school the next day only to be expelled for my "extra-curricular activities." I spent the next two weeks searching for pot. I found some, but then something miraculous happened.

After getting stoned, I laid in my bed listening to Pink Floyd's "Comfortably Numb." As I listened, I realized that God was in my room and that He loved me. The next day I asked God if I needed to continue smoking pot to find him. That night, my dad caught me smoking it again. They told me that I was to spend the night in their room, and they were taking me to rehab the next day. I told them what happened the night before and then burst into tears. My parents knelt down beside my couch, and I asked Jesus to come into my heart. This single experience completely changed my life.

Since this time, I have not been a perfect little angel. In fact, I have even gone back into a lot of the same things I was involved in before I asked Jesus to come into my heart. The Bible tells us that all have sinned and fallen short of the glory of God. There are no exceptions to this rule. Everyone who has put his or her trust in Jesus has failed morally at one point in time or another. This does not mean that they are going to hell, but they are human. However, I cannot say that going back to my old ways was okay. Proverbs tells us that as a dog returns to his vomit, so a fool returns to his folly (Proverbs 26:11). In conclusion I would say that it truly is amazing grace that saved a wretch like me.

Becoming a Christian

By MICAH W. GILES

October 19, 1998

The first major step in becoming a Christian is admitting that you are a sinner in need of a savior. In order to do this, one must understand first that "all have sinned and fall short of the glory of God." The idea that man is sinful is also presented by the English philosopher Thomas Hobbes who presented the idea of Natural Law, which states that man always acts out of self-interest, in his book *Leviathan*. Secondly, one must understand that "the wages of sin is death" or in other words, the wages of sin is eternal separation from God or Hell. In conjunction to this, one must understand that "God so loved mankind, He sent His son, Jesus Christ, to die a painful death on a cross for our behalf; and if we believe in Him, we will not have to face Hell, but will have eternal life" (John 3:16). In understanding the hopeless situation man is in without Christ, one can admit that he is a sinner in need of a savior.

The second major step to becoming a Christian is putting one's faith in Jesus to save one from his sins. The process of putting one's faith in Jesus is done by a simple prayer spoken in faith, for the Bible states that "if you confess with your mouth and believe with your heart that Jesus Christ is Lord then you shall be saved" (Romans 10:9). The Bible describes faith as "the assurance of things hoped for and the conviction of things not seen" (Hebrews 11:1). There is not an exact prescription for asking Jesus to save one's self. Many people have done it in different ways, but no matter how one does it, he must state four basic things: "I am a sinner," "I cannot get to heaven on my own," "I need God's help to get to heaven," and "believing in Jesus is the only way to get to God." Jesus said, "I am the way, the truth, and the life, no one comes to the Father but through me" (John 14:6). All God expects of us is to have "faith as the grain of a mustard seed." In relating this prayer to God through spoken word, unspoken word, or song, one commits his life into the hands of Christ. At this point, the life changes ownership.

Saying a simple prayer is not the fulfillment of becoming a Christian. Instead, this prayer is just the beginning of a whole new life. [First] Corinthians 6:20 states, "For you have been bought with a price: therefore, glorify God in your body." For those "who belong to Christ Jesus have crucified the flesh along with its passions and desires" which are "immorality, impurity, sensuality, idolatry, sorcery, enmities, strife, jealousy, outbursts of anger, disputes, dissensions, factions, envying, drunkenness, carousing, and things like these" (Galatians 5:19-21, 24), becoming a Christian does not mean that one will never sin again; it means, however, that we must continually strive to live a life that reflects the character of Christ. This type of life is achieved by a continuous repentance, or, as C.S. Lewis, a professor and author, writes in *Mere Christianity*, the process of "laying down your arms, surrendering, saying you are sorry, realizing that you have been on the wrong track and getting ready to start life over again from the ground floor" (Lewis p.59). In order to know what God expects of one's self and what he would have one do, one must read the Bible, which is the word of God which contains everything one needs to know on the Christian life. Moreover, God has given man direct access to him through prayer. In the same way that a person cannot have a relationship with another without speaking, neither can we have a relationship with God without conversation with Him through prayer. He even tells man to "present your requests" to Him (Philippians 4:6).

In summary, through repentance, the reading of God's Word, and prayer one can live this new life as a Christian.

Thomas Marshall

By MICAH W. GILES

Date Unknown
New Life Academy

Thomas Marshall is a seventeen-year-old young man who is a junior in high school. He has a younger sister and lives with his mom and dad. He does not say much, but inside I know he thinks the same thoughts we all do.

Thomas is also interested in basketball and fighter jets. I once asked him if he wanted to join the armed forces and fly fighters, and I was quite impressed with his response. He told me that he would love to, but he said that he did not know if that was what the Lord wanted him to do. He also has poor eyesight and is colorblind. Thomas has two sled cars that we call "the tanks." They probably weigh about five tons a piece. All in all I would conclude that Thomas is going to make it, and he will have a wonderful life.

My Concert Paper

By MICAH W. GILES

On Thursday, April 15, I was given the pleasure of attending one of the best piano recitals I have ever heard. The concert began at seven-thirty in the evening in the Delchamps Recital Hall at Huntingdon College. The concert hall was completely filled with people and anticipation. I was curious myself to find out why they had come to a relatively unpublicized piano concert. However, it was some of the sharpest piano playing I had ever heard. The two piano players Barbara and Ronald Shinn were outstanding. It was obvious that they were quite serious about their performance. They both played at the same time making it a Duet Recital. Being a piano player myself, I was absolutely fascinated at the sounds they were making. One piece I heard was the four-hand sonata written by Francis Poulenc. He wrote this piece at the age of nineteen. It was a very lively piece but had some contrasts in rhythm. It was faster in some parts than others. I liked it because it really displayed emotional feeling. I felt that the entire concert was a complete success. Standing ovations were given, myself included.

BIBLIOGRAPHY

Hobbes, Thomas. *Leviathan* . 1660. http://en.wikipedia. org/wiki/Thomas_Hobbes (accessed).

Lewis, C.S. *Mere Christianity*. MacMillan Publishing Company, 1944. http://en.wikipedia.org/wiki/Mere_ Christianity (accessed January 16, 2012).

Webster, Noah. *Trust—Definition*. New York, NY: S. Converse. Printed By Hezekiah Howe. New Haven, 1828. www.webster1828.com. (accessed January 16, 2012).